MORNING COFFEE

THE SIMPLE DAILY PRACTICE THAT TRANSFORMS EMOTIONAL OVERWHELM INTO SPIRITUAL FREEDOM

REVISED EDITION

QUINN PATH

Copyright © 2025 by Quinn Path

All rights reserved.

No part of this book may be reproduced in any form or by any electronic or mechanical means, including information storage and retrieval systems, without written permission from the author, except for the use of brief quotations in a book review.

CONTENTS

Introduction: The Gap Between Knowing and Being	1
Chapter 1: The Spiritual Seeking Traps	7
Chapter 2: The Ordinary Miracle	13
Chapter 3: The WEATHER Method Revealed	21
Chapter 4: W - Witness the Storm	31
Chapter 5: E - Explore the Landscape	44
Chapter 6: A - Accept the Weather	55
Chapter 7: T - Transition with Flow	68
Chapter 8: H - Harmonize Wisdom with Response	81
Chapter 9: E - Embody Natural Freedom	99
Chapter 10: R - Radiate Authentic Presence	109
Chapter 11: Workplace and Family Dynamics	120
Chapter 12: When Storms Return	132
Conclusion: Your Natural Freedom	148
After the Last Cup	157
Appendix A	159
Appendix B	163
Appendix C	170
Appendix D	176
Notes	185

INTRODUCTION: THE GAP BETWEEN KNOWING AND BEING

What if the pursuit of spiritual growth is actually keeping you trapped in suffering?

This question troubles many sincere seekers who have spent years learning about spirituality, yet still feel overwhelmed by emotions on an ordinary Tuesday afternoon. Maybe you see yourself here: the meditation teacher who loses patience in traffic, the mindfulness practitioner who feels anxious at work, or the consciousness enthusiast who can't sleep because their mind keeps racing, even though they know all about presence and non-attachment.

The Knowledge-Experience Gap in Real Life

Sarah's Story: After eight years as a respected meditation teacher, proficient in complex breathing techniques and the concept of non-attachment. However, when her father was diagnosed with cancer, she was overwhelmed by fear and grief, which shattered her inner peace. Instead of applying her tools, she fell into familiar patterns of panic and overwhelm, then added a layer of spiritual shame: "What kind of teacher gets this upset?"

Marcus's Dilemma: A corporate lawyer with fifteen years of mindfulness study, Marcus could maintain perfect equanimity during solo retreats. But five minutes into a partner meeting at his law firm, criticism from colleagues would trigger defensive reactions that lasted for hours. He knew intellectually that thoughts create suffering, but his emotional weather seemed entirely immune to his spiritual understanding.

Lisa's Frustration: A working mother who'd read every book on conscious parenting, Lisa could lecture about emotional control. At the same time, her teenagers' eye-rolling sent her into internal storms of hurt and anger. She understood that her children's behavior wasn't personal. Still, her nervous system responded as if every family conflict were a spiritual emergency.

These aren't stories of spiritual failure. Instead, they show the most common challenge for dedicated seekers: the gap between what you know and what you experience can leave you feeling like a fraud even after years of sincere practice.

The Performance Trap

You might recognize these symptoms of living in the gap:

The Spiritual Performance Anxiety: Feeling pressure to maintain a spiritual image while secretly struggling with the same old patterns. You monitor your responses during conversations to ensure you're being "enlightened" enough, which creates additional stress on top of whatever triggered you in the first place.

The Comparison Game: Measuring your inner chaos against others' curated spiritual personas on social media. Everyone else seems to have achieved the peace you're desperately seeking, leaving you wondering what is wrong with your practice.

The Fraud Syndrome: Knowing all the right concepts but feeling like a spiritual impostor when emotions overwhelm you. You can teach others about presence, but you can't access it when your boss criticizes your work or your partner triggers old wounds.

You are not broken, and you have not failed. The real issue is that you have been taught to look for awakening in places that don't really help.

The Ordinary Revolution

Modern spirituality often focuses on extraordinary states of consciousness, suggesting that awakening only comes from dramatic experiences like breakthrough meditation sessions, life-changing retreats, or mystical encounters that change everything. This focus on peak experiences leads to what I call 'experience hunting,' where you keep chasing the next high and overlook the lasting freedom found in everyday moments.

Consider the monastery student who spends twenty years seeking enlightenment through intense retreats, only to discover awakening while washing dishes. When the Zen master Huang Po taught, "Your everyday mind—that is the Way!" He wasn't encouraging complacency; he was pointing to the extraordinary nature of ordinary awareness when it's no longer taken for granted.

This revolutionary insight changes everything about how you approach spiritual development. Instead of waiting for the perfect conditions or extraordinary experiences, you can discover freedom through the simple act of drinking your morning coffee with complete presence.

The most profound awakening happens through ordinary moments, not extraordinary experiences.

Imagine waking up tomorrow and starting your day differently. Your morning coffee becomes a chance to be present, not because you are trying to make it spiritual, but because you notice what has always been there. When frustration comes up in traffic, rather than fighting it or judging yourself, you notice the feeling as it moves through your awareness, like the weather passing by.

The WEATHER Method: Your 28-Day Journey

What if emotions were not personal emergencies, but natural weather patterns? This simple shift in perspective can change everything. When you feel anger, instead of thinking "I'm angry" or "I shouldn't be angry," you might notice that "anger weather is passing through."

The WEATHER Method emerged from this recognition—a seven-step framework that teaches you to work with emotional weather in the same way meteorologists work with atmospheric conditions: through observation, understanding, and skillful response rather than control.

W - Witness - Learning to observe emotions without immediate reaction.

E - Explore - Investigate emotional patterns with curiosity instead of judgment.

A - Accept - Accepting emotions as natural weather patterns.

T - Transition - Working with the natural rhythm of emotional movement.

H - Harmonize - Translating emotional wisdom into mindful response.

E - Embody - Making emotional freedom your natural state.

R - Radiate - Expressing genuine presence in relationships.

What You'll Learn: Your 28-Day Transformation

Week 1: Foundation Building

• Master the 5-second pause that creates space between trigger and response.

• Develop basic emotional weather vocabulary.

• Learn to distinguish between feeling emotions and being controlled by them.

• Practice simple acceptance phrases that stop internal fighting.

Week 2: Deepening Awareness

• Build sophisticated emotional pattern recognition.

• Develop curiosity-based exploration that reveals emotional wisdom.

• Learn to work with natural emotional timing rather than forcing resolution.

• Practice staying present during moderate emotional storms.

Week 3: Natural Integration

• Transform emotional experiences into practical decision-making guidance.

- Apply the method seamlessly during workplace stress and family interactions.

- Develop your ability to handle any emotional weather.

- Begin radiating an authentic presence without spiritual performance.

Week 4: Embodied Freedom

- Experience emotional freedom as your natural state rather than an achievement.

- Support others' emotional well-being without taking on their problems.

- Integrate all seven steps into unconscious competence.

- Live from embodied wisdom rather than seeking mode.

Your Ordinary Enlightenment

The coffee cup you hold right now offers more potential for awakening than any exotic spiritual practice. The goal is not to reach a perfect state of constant calm, but to build the wisdom and resilience to handle whatever emotional weather comes your way.

The sense of integration you are seeking is not something you will find in a future achievement. It is available to you right now, regardless of the emotions you are experiencing. As you drink your morning coffee, you have another chance to notice the ordinary miracle of awakening that has always been right in front of you. The gap between knowing and being is about to close, not by gaining more spiritual knowledge, but by finally learning to live the wisdom you already have.

CHAPTER 1: THE SPIRITUAL SEEKING TRAPS

Even after years of spiritual study, you might still feel like an impostor. You know the language, understand the concepts, and can even teach others, but you may not feel truly enlightened or consistently at peace. This feeling, sometimes called the Spiritual Fraud Complex, is common among those who take their practice seriously. It adds to your original emotional challenges and can leave you feeling tired, wishing you were further along.

The Knowledge Trap That Keeps Smart People Stuck

If you're reading this book, you're probably intelligent, well-educated, and interested in complex ideas. These strengths can sometimes hold you back in spiritual growth because they make it easy to try to think your way to freedom instead of feeling your way there.

Think about it: you wouldn't learn to swim just by reading about water, studying stroke techniques, or watching Olympic swimmers. You get in the water and practice. Yet, most people try to master their emotions by thinking about them instead of experiencing them directly.

Intelligence can get in the way of spiritual growth when you rely on analysis instead of direct experience.

Your analytical mind excels at:

- Comparing different spiritual approaches.

- Understanding complex philosophical concepts.

- Identifying patterns in your behavior.

- Planning ideal spiritual practices.

But it struggles with:

- Staying present during emotional intensity.

- Accepting what is rather than analyzing why.

- Trusting natural processes over mental control.

- Integrating insights into automatic responses.

This leads to a unique kind of educated helplessness, a special kind that comes from knowing a lot. You know resisting your feelings causes suffering, but you still do it. You understand emotions will pass, but you still get caught up in them. You may know the present moment has everything you need, but you find yourself thinking about the past and the future more.

Retreats can give you powerful experiences and important insights, but they can also make it seem like real change only happens in special moments. In reality, transformation often takes place in the small, everyday moments of life.

This Peak Experience Trap manifests in several ways:

Spiritual Tourism: You chase experiences rather than develop skills. Each retreat, workshop, or ceremony becomes another attempt to capture that transformative moment that will finally set everything right.

State Dependency: You believe peaceful states indicate spiritual progress while difficult emotions signal failure. This creates an internal war against natural emotional responses.

Ordinary Avoidance: Daily emotional challenges become obstacles to spirituality rather than opportunities for it. You postpone dealing with practical issues until you're "more conscious."

The most profound spiritual masters found freedom not through extraordinary experiences, but by fully accepting the ordinary ones. They realized something that is often overlooked today: the extraordinary is found within the ordinary, not apart from it.

The Violence of Spiritual Self-Improvement

Most people think of violence as something obvious, like shouting, fighting, or physical harm. But in spiritual circles, there's a quieter kind of violence: the urge to fix, change, or improve your emotional state. This hidden pressure can make you feel like who you are right now isn't good enough.

Violence #1: The Emotional Police Force

You might develop an inner system that is always on the lookout for so-called negative emotions. As soon as anger, fear, or sadness shows up, this inner police force jumps in with spiritual techniques to bring back positive feelings. This approach turns your relationship with your emotions into a struggle, as if you are fighting against the natural parts of yourself.

Violence #2: The Spiritual Bypass

When difficult emotions arise, you quickly deploy spiritual concepts to avoid fully experiencing them. "Everything happens for a reason," "I'm choosing love over fear," or "This is just ego" become escape routes from authentic emotional experience.

Violence #3: The Improvement Treadmill

You keep pushing yourself to become a better version of who you are, which often means you are always running away from your current self.

Liberating Yourself with Bold Allowance

You don't avoid these spiritual traps by using better techniques or stricter discipline. Instead, it's about accepting your humanity as you walk your spiritual path.

When you feel anger, it might just mean your boundaries have been crossed, not that you need more patience. When you feel sadness, it may be genuine grief for a loss that deserves recognition, not a sign that you lack gratitude. When you feel anxious, it doesn't mean you don't trust the universe; it's just a normal response to uncertainty.

Allow yourself to be imperfect in your practice.

Missing meditation sessions doesn't make you a bad practitioner; it just means you're human and your needs change. If your mind wanders during practice, it's not a problem to fix, but a chance to practice bringing your attention back.

Permit yourself to always be a beginner

Maybe spiritual mastery isn't about reaching perfection, but about building a better relationship with imperfection. The most advanced practitioners might not be those who never struggle, but those who face their struggles with awareness and compassion.

Knowledge Trap Self-Assessment

Rate how often you experience these patterns (1 = Never, 5 = Constantly):

• **Knowledge Without Application:** You understand spiritual concepts but struggle to apply them during emotional challenges ___

• **Spiritual Performance:** You monitor your responses to ensure you're being "enlightened" enough ___

• **Seeking Addiction:** You constantly search for new techniques, teachers, or insights ___

• **Peak Experience Dependence:** You judge your spiritual progress by the intensity of your experiences ___

• **Ordinary Moment Dismissal:** You consider daily life less spiritual than formal practice ___

• **Emotional Resistance:** You treat difficult emotions as spiritual failures ___

• **Teacher Comparison:** You feel inadequate compared to apparently more advanced practitioners ___

Scoring:

• 7-14: Minimal trap patterns - you're likely integrating well

• 15-25: Moderate trap patterns - awareness will help you break free

- 26-35: Significant trap patterns - this book will be particularly valuable

Your Knowledge Is Not Wasted

Before we go on, let's address a common worry: "If more knowledge isn't the answer, did I waste years learning?" Not at all. Everything you've learned is valuable. Your insights and techniques become useful when you put them into practice, not just collect them.

Think of it like this: you've spent years gathering ingredients for a meal. The issue isn't the quality of what you have, but that you haven't learned to cook yet. The next chapters will help you use what you already have, instead of searching for more.

Your spiritual knowledge provides the foundation for practical application. Understanding non-dual awareness helps you recognize the space between stimulus and response. Learning about impermanence supports you during difficult emotions. Studying mindfulness provides you with tools for present-moment awareness.

The real issue was never your knowledge. It's that you didn't have practical ways to use it during real-life emotional challenges, not just during perfect meditation sessions.

The spiritual seeking traps dissolve when you stop treating emotions as obstacles to overcome. It starts to fade when you stop seeing emotions as problems to fix and start viewing them as weather to move through. The goal isn't permanent peace, but learning how to handle whatever comes up inside you.

CHAPTER 2: THE ORDINARY MIRACLE

Your most profound spiritual breakthrough awaits in this morning's cup of coffee. This isn't another metaphor designed to make you feel better about your seemingly mundane existence—it's a literal truth that contradicts everything the spiritual marketplace has taught you about where awakening lives. While you've been searching for extraordinary experiences to validate your spiritual progress, the very ordinariness you've been trying to transcend contains more awakening potential than any retreat, workshop, or intensive practice you've ever encountered.

The Coffee Revelation

Morning coffee doesn't require special conditions. Unlike meditation retreats that demand weeks away from responsibilities, perfect silence, or ideal circumstances, your daily coffee ritual happens regardless of your mood, the weather, or how well you slept. This accessibility makes it more reliable for spiritual development than any practice that depends on external arrangements.

You've likely experienced this yourself without recognizing its significance. Think about those moments when you're completely present with your morning routine—feeling the warmth of the mug in your hands, noticing the steam rising, experiencing the first taste without thinking about your to-do list. These aren't lesser spiritual experiences because they happen in your kitchen rather than on a mountain. They're actually more spiritually significant because they demonstrate that presence doesn't require special locations or circumstances.

Imagine holding your coffee mug right now. Feel its weight in your hands. Notice the temperature seeping through the ceramic into your palms. Watch the steam curling and dispersing upward with each slight movement of air. Breathe in the aroma, not the idea of coffee, but this specific scent in this exact moment. As you take your first sip, feel the liquid's warmth spreading across your tongue, followed by a slight bitterness and whatever subtle flavors emerge as it settles.

This sensory experience contains everything that mystics have pointed toward for centuries: complete presence with what is actually happening right now. The warmth you're feeling is as profound as any mystical vision. The simple act of tasting without mental commentary is as powerful as any advanced meditation technique.

Why Convenience Equals Spiritual Depth

Consistency trumps intensity in spiritual development. A meditation retreat might provide profound insights for a week, but your morning coffee ritual offers countless opportunities for presence every single day for years and years.

The retreat model creates what researchers call "peak-end bias"—you remember the most intense moment and how it ended, but you struggle to integrate the insights into daily life[1]. Your coffee ritual eliminates this integration challenge because it happens within the context where you need the spiritual skills most: ordinary daily life.

Real spiritual development happens through repetition, not revelation. While dramatic breakthroughs capture attention, sustainable freedom emerges through countless small moments of conscious presence accumulated over time. Your morning routine provides this repetition naturally, without forcing you to maintain motivation for elaborate practices.

The Mystics Who Found Freedom in Simplicity

Revolutionary mystics consistently found freedom in simple, daily moments rather than in extraordinary experiences.

Rumi wrote his most beloved poetry while observing ordinary Persian life—bakers kneading bread, children playing in courtyards, lovers meeting in gardens. His famous verse, "Let yourself be silently drawn by the strange pull of what you really love." emerged not from dramatic, mystical experiences, but from observing his responses to simple, daily pleasures[2].

The Zen master, Joshu, achieved enlightenment while drinking tea. When students asked him about the nature of Buddha, he famously replied, "Have some tea." This wasn't cryptic spiritual bypassing—it was pointing directly to the awakened awareness available in the simple act of conscious consumption[3].

Thich Nhat Hanh spent decades teaching "mindful coffee drinking" as a complete spiritual practice. He demonstrated that full presence, even with something as simple as drinking tea, could deliver the same awakening insights as years of formal meditation practice[4].

What if You Don't Drink Coffee?

The coffee metaphor represents *any* routine activity that engages your senses without requiring complex preparation. If coffee isn't part of your life, the same principle applies to:

• **Morning tea:** The ritual of steeping, the steam, the gradual color change in your cup.

• **Breakfast preparation:** Feeling fruit in your hands, hearing the sizzle of eggs, smelling the toast.

• **Showering:** Feeling water on your skin, the scent of soap, and steam filling the bathroom.

• **Getting dressed:** The texture of fabrics, the ritual of preparation, the act of looking in the mirror.

• **Morning walk:** Feeling your feet on the ground, breathing the outdoor air, and noticing light.

The key isn't any specific activity—it's choosing one routine morning experience and treating it as your laboratory for presence practice. The miracle lives in the *attention* you bring, not in the object of attention.

The Emotional Weather Connection

Every emotion that arises during your morning coffee is a perfect doorway to presence. This reframe alone revolutionizes your relationship with difficult emotions because it eliminates the need to have only positive emotional experiences during spiritual practice.

Suppose you feel irritated while drinking your coffee because you're running late. In that case, that irritation becomes your spiritual practice rather than an obstacle. Instead of thinking "I can't be present because I'm irritated," you learn to recognize that "I can be present with this irritation." The emotion becomes the object of awareness rather than a distraction from awareness. One of my meditation teachers used to say, "Don't tell yourself to be patient, just watch the impatience!"

This approach works with human psychology rather than against it. Traditional spiritual approaches often require cultivating special emotional states—such as inner peace, loving kindness, and equanimity—before practicing effectively. The ordinary moment approach meets you wherever you are emotionally and uses that emotional reality as the foundation for practice.

Your morning emotional state becomes the perfect raw material for developing emotional freedom:

- **Feeling rushed?** Practice presence with urgency without trying to eliminate it.

- **Feeling tired?** Practice awareness of fatigue without requiring yourself to feel energized.

- **Feeling anxious about the day ahead?** Practice witnessing anxiety without needing to feel calm.

- **Feeling grateful and peaceful?** Practice awareness of pleasant emotions without clinging to them.

The Revolutionary Reframe: Emotions as Weather

. . .

Emotions are weather patterns, not personal emergencies. This single reframe changes everything about how you relate to your inner experience because it removes the urgency that creates emotional suffering.

When you check the weather forecast and see rain predicted, you don't take it personally. You don't spend energy trying to change the forecast or blame yourself for not creating sunshine. You simply note the weather pattern and adjust your plans accordingly. This same natural response can be applied to emotional weather.

Consider how you currently relate to emotions versus how you relate to the physical weather:

Difficult Emotions	Physical Weather
Take them personally	Accept as natural phenomena
Judge as "bad" or "wrong"	Recognize as temporary conditions
Try to control	Respond appropriately
Are obstacles to happiness	To work with, rather than against
Feel responsible for creating	Understand as part of natural cycles

The weather metaphor creates emotional freedom through natural acceptance. Just as you don't try to stop rain by force of will, you can learn to experience emotional storms without trying to stop them through mental effort. Just as you trust that storms will pass naturally, you can develop confidence that emotional intensity will change without your intervention.

Your Coffee Practice Begins Now

. . .

Your coffee drinking becomes a complete emotional freedom training program. Each element of the experience offers specific practice opportunities that build the skills you need for working with emotions, such as weather patterns:

Witnessing Practice: Notice the physical sensations of holding the warm mug, the sound of liquid pouring, the sight of rising steam—all without trying to change or improve the experience.

Emotional Weather Awareness: When emotions arise during coffee drinking, approach them with curiosity rather than trying to eliminate them immediately. If anxiety surfaces about your day ahead, note: "Ah, anxiety weather is here with my coffee this morning."

Acceptance Practice: Allow whatever emotional weather is present while drinking your coffee, welcoming irritation as readily as contentment. You might silently say: "This frustration is welcome at my breakfast table."

Natural Flow Practice: Notice how emotions naturally change during the coffee ritual without forcing. You might begin with grogginess and end with alertness, or start with peace and notice concerns arising—all of this is a natural part of the weather.

This isn't about making coffee drinking into another spiritual performance. You're not trying to have a perfect presence or ideal emotions during your morning routine. You're simply using whatever naturally occurs during this ordinary activity as raw material for developing emotional insight.

Try this right now with your next cup: Before taking your first sip, pause for three seconds and notice what you're feeling emotionally. Don't try to change it—acknowledge whatever weather is present. Take your first sip while staying aware of both the coffee's taste and your emotional state. Notice how the simple act of conscious attention transforms an ordinary moment into something alive with presence.

Beyond the Coffee Cup

The principles that make coffee drinking spiritually powerful can be applied to every ordinary activity. Brushing teeth, taking showers, walking to your car, washing dishes—each of these routine activities contains the same awakening potential as your morning coffee ritual.

This realization expands your spiritual practice from a few minutes per day to dozens of opportunities throughout every day. Instead of trying to find time for spiritual practice, you discover that your entire life is already structured as a spiritual practice waiting to be recognized.

Your ordinary life becomes your spiritual path. This isn't a consolation prize for people who can't access "real" spiritual practices—it's the most efficient and sustainable approach to spiritual development available. When you develop emotional freedom through ordinary activities, you know the skills will work during ordinary challenges because they've been tested in ordinary circumstances from the beginning.

The transition from seeking extraordinary experiences to recognizing ordinary ones requires a fundamental shift in how you define spiritual progress. You'll learn to measure progress by your ability to remain present during routine activities and how gracefully you handle emotional weather during ordinary moments, not by how often you feel blissful.

CHAPTER 3: THE WEATHER METHOD REVEALED

The simplest solutions are often hidden behind the most complex problems. Feeling emotionally overwhelmed does not mean you have failed spiritually; it is just like weather moving through your inner sky. Just as meteorologists learn to read the weather, you can learn to notice, understand, and work with your emotional climate instead of being carried away by every storm.

The Framework That Changes Everything

For years, you may have gathered spiritual ideas like souvenirs from a trip you have not fully experienced. You know about presence, non-attachment, and acceptance, but when Monday morning anxiety or Sunday evening dread shows up, all that wisdom can feel far away. This does not mean you are doing anything wrong. It simply means you need a way to connect understanding with real experience.

The WEATHER Method provides that bridge.

This seven-step framework transforms abstract spiritual concepts into practical daily experiences. Each letter represents a distinct approach to working with emotional energy, and together they form a comprehensive system for achieving lasting emotional freedom. The beauty lies not in the individual steps, but in how they work together as an integrated whole:

W - Witness the Storm

E - Explore the Landscape

A - Accept the Weather

T - Transition with Flow

H - Harmonize Wisdom with Response

E - Embody Natural Freedom

R - Radiate Authentic Presence

Why Weather Works Where Other Methods Fail

Your mind often finds metaphors easier to relate to than abstract ideas. If you tell yourself to "accept your anger," you might resist because acceptance can seem passive or weak. But if you think of anger as a thunderstorm moving through your inner sky, your perspective can change. You would not take a thunderstorm personally or try to bargain with it; you would simply notice it and respond as needed.

This meteorological approach works because it is something we can all easily relate to. You already know how to deal with the external weather. You check the conditions, dress appropriately, and adjust your plans when necessary. You wouldn't waste energy resenting rain or arguing with snow. This same natural wisdom can be applied to your inner climate.

Morning Coffee

The weather metaphor helps you step back from your emotions without feeling cut off from them. You can watch your feelings with the same curiosity you have when you look at clouds in the sky. This way of seeing things gives you space, which is the important gap between what happens and how you respond. That space lets you choose your actions rather than just react automatically.

The Scientific Foundation

Modern neuroscience supports what contemplative traditions have said for centuries: emotions are temporary chemical events, not the lasting parts of who you are. Dr. Jill Bolte Taylor's research shows that the physical aspect of an emotion —the chemical surge in your body —usually lasts about 90 seconds. Emotions last longer only when you keep thinking about them. If you resist, analyze, or dwell on your feelings, you make them stick around for much longer[1].

The WEATHER Method works with this natural emotional rhythm rather than against it. By learning to observe without interfering, you allow emotions to unfold naturally and without hindrance.

The Complete WEATHER Framework

W - Witness the Storm (5-30 seconds)

In this "bare" witnessing phase, you practice noticing your emotions as they come up, simply and honestly, without jumping in or reacting right away. Even small expectations or worries can change how you see things, so try to observe without judgment. This is how you find out what is really happening. With practice, you can stay calm and clear, even when strong emotions feel like crashing waves; you can maintain a sense of calm and objectivity.

Key Practice: The 5-second pause between feeling and responding.

Common Mistake: Analyzing emotions, rather than just observing them.

E - Explore the Landscape (30 seconds - 2 minutes)

Every emotion conveys essential information. They should be seen as messengers offering valuable insights, not just problems to be solved. For instance, anger may signal a violation of personal boundaries, sadness can indicate a need for connection, and anxiety often highlights areas where you feel unprepared or uncertain.

Core Skill: Investigating emotional patterns with curiosity.

Key Practice: Shift from "How do I get rid of this?" to "What is this telling me?"

Common Mistake: Over-analyzing emotions instead of experiencing them directly.

A - Accept the Weather (Immediate and ongoing)

Acceptance is often the hardest and the most powerful step in the WEATHER Method. It is not about giving up or ignoring your feelings. Instead, it means actively allowing your emotions to be just as they are, without feeling you must fix, change, or improve them.

Core Skill: Welcoming emotions as natural phenomena.

Key Practice: Saying "This [emotion] is welcome here" without trying to fix it.

Common Mistake: Confusing acceptance with liking or wanting the emotion.

T - Transition with Flow (Variable timing)

To work with your emotions in a healthy way, you need to be patient and trust that feelings will change in their own time. Many people try to force their emotions to go away by pushing through sadness, fighting anxiety, or hurrying past anger. This usually creates more tension inside and can make tough feelings last longer.

Emotions follow their own timing and rhythm: grief comes in waves that you cannot predict or control, anger needs to settle before you can think clearly, and anxiety often has to be felt fully before it can turn into useful caution.

Core Skill: Working with natural emotional rhythms.

Key Practice: Allowing emotions to move without forcing premature resolution.

Common Mistake: Trying to control the timing of emotional movement.

H - Harmonize Wisdom with Response (1-5 minutes)

. . .

The fifth step turns your emotional experiences into useful wisdom for daily life. Instead of viewing emotions as problems that get in the way, you start to see them as helpful guides for making good choices. Your emotional weather becomes the inner compass, helping you to make decisions based on real understanding rather than following old habits.

Core Skill: Using emotional information to guide wise action.

Key Practice: Making decisions based on emotional wisdom plus practical needs.

Common Mistake: Acting impulsively on every emotional impulse.

E - Embody Natural Freedom

The sixth step is about moving from practicing emotional freedom as a skill to living it as a natural part of who you are. You may not always feel perfect, but you gain the confidence to handle whatever emotional challenges may come your way.

When you truly embody emotional freedom, it becomes a natural part of your life. You no longer have to think about using the WEATHER Method. It feels as easy and automatic as breathing, and you respond to emotions without extra effort.

Core Skill: Living emotional freedom as your natural state.

Key Practice: Seamlessly integrating the method into daily life.

Common Mistake: Making emotional freedom into another spiritual identity.

R - Radiate Authentic Presence (Natural and effortless)

The final step takes your emotional freedom beyond just helping yourself to supporting others. This is not about teaching or preaching to anyone. Instead, it is about living with such peace and honesty that others feel inspired to find their own emotional freedom.

When you are no longer ruled by your emotions, you become a steady presence for those around you. Others notice your calm and often feel more at ease when they are with you. This doesn't require any effort on your part; it is simply what happens when you live with emotional freedom.

Core Skill: Sharing your stability through authentic being.

Key Practice: Modeling healthy emotional expression without preaching.

Common Mistake: Trying to teach or fix others' emotional patterns.

Progression Through the WEATHER Steps

Beginner Stage (Weeks 1-2): Focus on W and E

Learn to pause before you react and start getting curious about your emotions. You do not need to master acceptance or integration right away. Just focus on noticing and exploring your emotional weather.

Developing Stage (Weeks 3-4): Add A and T

Start practicing acceptance, but do not try to force it. Notice the natural timing of your emotions. Some days these skills will come easily, and on other days they might seem harder. This is completely normal.

Integration Stage (Weeks 5-8): Emphasize H and the first E

Start using emotional information to guide decisions. Begin integrating the method into daily routines. The steps will start to flow more naturally as time goes by.

Embodiment Stage (Weeks 9+): Natural R expression

As you improve, you'll find yourself feeling more emotionally free without even trying. Sure, old habits might pop up now and then, but you'll bounce back with kindness toward yourself.

The Weather Method Flow Chart

EMOTIONAL TRIGGER
  ↓
W: WITNESS (5-30 seconds)
  - 5-second pause
  - Notice without reaction
  ↓
E: EXPLORE (30 seconds - 2 minutes)
  - Ask: "What is this telling me?"
  - Investigate objectively
  ↓
A: ACCEPT (Immediate)
  - Welcome the emotion

- Let go of the need to fix things.

↓

T: TRANSITION (Variable timing)

 - Allow natural movement

 - Trust emotional timing

↓

H: HARMONIZE (1-5 minutes)

 - Use emotion as guidance

 - Make informed decision

↓

E: EMBODY (Ongoing)

 - Live from natural freedom

 - Integrate seamlessly

↓

R: RADIATE (Effortless)

 - Model authentic presence

 - Serve through being

The WEATHER Method becomes truly powerful when it integrates seamlessly into your ordinary activities. Rather than creating special times for emotional practice, you learn to use every moment as an opportunity for deeper presence.

Start small by working with whatever emotions you are feeling right now. Don't wait for everything to feel calm before you begin, because difficult moments often teach you the most.

Emotional challenges are the best way to practice the WEATHER Method.

Start with:

- Practice the five-second pause during minor irritations.

- Notice body sensations during routine activities.

- Experiment with accepting one difficult emotion per day.

- Use simple emotional weather language to describe your inner state.

Emotional freedom grows through steady, incremental steps rather than big breakthroughs. Every time you pause before reacting, choose curiosity over judgment, or accept a tough emotion, you strengthen your ability to feel free in the long term.

Track your progress not by the absence of difficult emotions, but by your changing relationship to them. Notice when you recover more quickly from emotional storms, when you feel less controlled by moods, and when you respond more consciously to challenging situations.

The next chapters will walk you through each step of the WEATHER Method, offering practical exercises, real-life examples, and help for common challenges. You will learn to handle anger, anxiety, sadness, fear, and joy as weather patterns, not personal flaws. Most importantly, you will discover how to trust your natural emotional wisdom rather than rely on external methods or teachers for inner peace.

You don't need the perfect conditions or special situations to begin your journey toward emotional freedom. All it takes is a willingness to meet your emotions with the same acceptance you use for the weather outside. The change you are looking for is not waiting in the future; it is available to you right now, in whatever emotions you are feeling.

CHAPTER 4: W - WITNESS THE STORM

Between an emotional trigger and your response, there's a world of possibilities.

This small pause—the space between what happens to you and how you respond—can be more powerful than years of spiritual searching. Most people go through life without ever noticing this hidden gap, caught up in automatic emotional reactions. But this space is always there, in every emotional experience, patiently waiting for you to pay attention.

The moment you start noticing your emotional storms instead of being swept away by them, you begin to experience real freedom.

The Revolutionary 5-Second Pause

Emotional freedom begins with a simple, conscious choice that takes just five seconds. After something triggers you, there is a brief window to decide how you will respond. This idea is not just mystical; neuroscience supports it. Your brain's emotional center reacts first, sending chemical signals through your body. For about five seconds, your conscious mind has a chance to step in before old habits take over.

Many spiritual people miss this window because they expect something dramatic or complicated. They think witnessing their emotions should feel profound or require a special setting. In reality, the 5-second pause is refreshingly simple:

When you notice an emotional reaction beginning:

• **Pause your body**—stop whatever physical movement you were about to make.

• **Take one conscious breath**—not a deep-breathing technique, just one intentional breath.

• **Feel the physical sensations**—scan your body to find where you feel the emotion.

• **Ask one question**—"What's here right now?"

• **Choose your response**—act from a place of awareness rather than simply reacting.

This isn't about stuffing down your emotions or pretending you don't care. It's about giving yourself a little space, so you can choose how to respond instead of letting your reactions run the show.

Practice Integration Points

The best thing about the 5-second pause is that you can use it anytime, right in the middle of your daily life. You do not need to set up perfect conditions:

Morning coffee preparation: when you feel the first stirrings of daily anxiety or overwhelm.

Email checking: before responding to challenging messages.

Doorway crossings: using physical transitions as emotional check-in points.

Traffic encounters: when other drivers trigger frustration.

Workplace interactions: before responding to criticism or challenging requests.

Workplace Example: Sarah, a marketing executive, discovered the effectiveness of this approach during team meetings. When her boss set unrealistic deadlines, she experienced a familiar surge of defensive anger. Instead of immediately protesting, she paused for five seconds. "I can feel myself wanting to argue," she said to herself, "but what if I just listened first?" This simple pause allowed her to hear the underlying pressure her boss was facing and respond with solutions rather than defensiveness.

Body-Scanning for Emotional Intelligence

Your body acts as an emotional guidance system, sending you signals through sensations, not just thoughts. Many of us think about emotions as ideas, like saying, "I feel angry" or "I'm sad," without noticing what is actually happening in our bodies. When you are stuck in your head, you miss the real, physical signs your emotions give you. Body-scanning for emotions changes this. By noticing how anger appears in your shoulders, anxiety in your stomach, or grief in your chest, you start to catch the early warning signs, often before your emotions become overwhelming.

. . .

QUINN PATH

The Basic Body-Scan Technique

This practice takes less than thirty seconds and can be done anywhere:

Starting from your head, pay attention to any physical sensations, such as pressure or tension, on your scalp. Next, focus on your face, ears, and jaw. After that, shift your attention to your neck and throat, noticing any feelings or sensations there. Continue down the body to your shoulders, chest, abdomen, and back, then down both arms and fingers. Finally, shift your focus to the rest of your body: acknowledge any sensations that arise in the same way.

Common Emotional Signatures

Emotion	Physical Location	Typical Sensations
Anger	Chest, shoulders, jaw	Heat, tension, clenched feeling
Anxiety	Stomach, throat	Butterflies, tightness, shallow breathing
Sadness	Chest, behind the eyes	Heaviness, aching, an empty feeling
Fear	Stomach, legs	Cold, trembling, urge to flee
Excitement	Chest, arms	Warmth, energy, expansion
Shame	Shoulders, head	Sinking, wanting to hide
Joy	Heart, whole body	Lightness, expansion, warmth

Remember, these are just general patterns. Your emotional signature might be different, and that's perfectly normal. The goal isn't to match a standard template but to become intimately familiar with your unique emotional landscape.

Creating Natural Emotion Check-Ins

The most powerful spiritual practices happen in ordinary moments, not just in special circumstances. Traditional spiritual approaches often require dedicated time, meditation cushions, quiet spaces, and uninterrupted periods. While these can be helpful, they often create a separation between 'spiritual time' and 'ordinary life.' This can reinforce the gap between what you know and what you experience.

Natural emotion check-ins dissolve this separation by weaving awareness into activities you're already doing. Instead of adding more tasks to your spiritual to-do list, you engage in the existing routines with mindful presence.

Morning Coffee Awareness

Your morning coffee ritual contains profound potential for emotional witnessing. The routine nature makes it perfect for establishing consistent awareness practices without feeling forced or artificial.

The 3-Sip practice:

• **First sip:** Check in with your physical state, such as your energy level, tension, and overall body sensation.

- **Second sip:** Notice your emotional weather—what feelings are present right now without trying to change them.

- **Third sip:** Set an intention to stay emotionally aware throughout the day. Do not force anything; just remain curious.

This requires no extra time or special equipment. You're simply bringing consciousness to an activity you would be doing anyway.

Walking Meditation Integration

As you walk to your vehicle, between workplace buildings, or climb the stairs, these moments provide natural opportunities for emotional awareness.

The Footstep Method

- **First few steps:** Notice your breathing pattern and walking rhythm.

- **Middle steps:** Scan your body for emotional information.

- **Final steps:** Ask yourself, "What is my emotional weather right now?"

Workplace Transition Points

Modern work provides countless natural check-in opportunities:

- **Before opening emails:** Take one conscious breath and scan for emotional states.

- **While the phone is loading:** Use those few seconds for body awareness.

- **During elevator rides:** Quick emotional weather check instead of scrolling mindlessly.

- **At red traffic lights:** Brief emotional presence practice.

The Doorway Practice

Physical doorways offer perfect prompts for emotional awareness. Each threshold crossing becomes an invitation to witness your internal state.

Simple Doorway Protocol

- **Pause at the threshold**: One foot on each side of the doorway.

- **Take inventory:** Quick body scan and emotional check-in.

- **Choose your energy**: Decide how you want to enter this new space.

- **Cross mindfully**: Step through with conscious presence.

Example: Lisa, a busy mother of three, initially resisted formal meditation because she "couldn't find the time." But doorway practices revolutionized her relationship with emotional awareness. "I walk through dozens of doorways daily," she realized. "Suddenly, I had dozens of opportunities for presence practice. My kids even started noticing when I'd pause at doorways, and eventually, they began doing it too."

Common Witnessing Obstacles

Understanding common challenges helps you handle them skillfully rather than being derailed by them.

"I Don't Have The Time"

Many spiritually advanced seekers think emotional witnessing takes a lot of time. This misunderstanding keeps them stuck in the seeking mode, always waiting for the right moment to start.

The practices in this chapter don't need any extra time. You're just becoming aware of activities you're already doing, not adding new tasks to your busy schedule.

"It's Not Working"

When people first try emotional witnessing, they often expect quick, dramatic results. If they still feel angry, sad, or anxious while practicing, they assume they're doing something wrong.

Witnessing doesn't remove emotions—it transforms how you relate to them. Success isn't about avoiding tough feelings but about staying present with whatever comes up.

"I Forgot to Practice"

Consistency challenges are completely normal, especially in the early stages. Most people forget to practice witnessing until they are already caught in emotional reactions.

Start with something small. Choose a specific trigger, like the sound of your phone notifications, as your cue to practice witnessing. Every time you hear it, take one conscious breath. Once this becomes a habit, you can add more.

"I'm Too Emotional"

Some people believe they're "too sensitive" or "too emotional" to make witnessing practices work. They assume emotional intensity disqualifies them from developing emotional mastery.

Emotional sensitivity is actually an advantage for witnessing. You notice emotional changes more easily, which gives you more information for awareness practices. You don't need to become less emotional; you just need to become more skilled at working with your emotions.

. . .

Building Your Personal Witnessing Style

Effective emotional witnessing fits your natural personality and lifestyle, rather than forcing you into a set mold. The techniques here are a starting point, but your practice will develop its own style based on your temperament, schedule, and preferences.

For Analytical Types

If you naturally gravitate toward systems and data, consider:

- Emotional tracking apps: Use technology to help you develop awareness.

- Pattern analysis: Keep simple logs of your emotional triggers and responses.

- Metrics approach: Track small improvements in your reaction time or emotional intensity.

For Creative Types

If you're drawn to artistic or intuitive approaches:

- Emotional journaling: Write briefly and creatively about your emotional state.

- Movement practices: Add body awareness to your stretching or exercise routines.

- Artistic expression: Use drawing or music as ways to witness your emotions.

For Busy Professionals

If your schedule is packed with obligations:

- Technology integration: Use phone alerts as reminders to practice witnessing.

- Commute practices: Build awareness during your travel time.

- Meeting mastery: Use professional interactions as opportunities to practice awareness.

Marcus, a software engineer, found that his stomach would begin to churn five minutes before entering networking events. He didn't just brush off his feelings as nerves; he saw them as helpful signals. So, he started showing up early and looked for a cozy spot to practice a little 5-second pause, really listening to his body. "Instead of battling my anxiety, I began to embrace it as useful info," he shared. "It turns out my body was just trying to help me get ready for social moments!"

The Minimum Practice

If you're feeling overwhelmed by the various techniques presented, then just start with one approach:

- Choose your daily anchor activity: pick something you do every single day without exception (making coffee, brushing your teeth, checking your phone first thing in the morning).

- Add one awareness element: during this activity, notice your emotional state without trying to change it.

- Practice for one week: commit to this minimal practice for seven days.

- Evaluate and expand: after one week, decide whether to add another element or try a different approach.

This approach honors your sophisticated spiritual background while respecting your practical limitations.

. . .

QUINN PATH

The Ripple Effects of Witnessing

As emotional witnessing becomes natural, its effects extend well beyond your personal emotional experience. The ability to stay present with difficult emotions while keeping perspective leads to profound changes in all areas of life:

Professional Transformation: Workplace dynamics change significantly when you stop reacting instinctively to stress, criticism, or difficult colleagues. You start responding with clarity rather than defensiveness, which often enhances professional relationships and opportunities.

Relationship Healing: Friends and family often see increased emotional openness and less reactivity. This allows for more genuine connections and can repair longstanding relationship patterns.

Decision-Making Clarity: When emotions provide insight instead of dictating responses, decision-making becomes clearer. You can feel angry about a situation yet still choose wise actions or acknowledge fear while moving forward anyway.

Physical Health Benefits: Chronic emotional reactivity causes ongoing stress in the body. As witnessing becomes more natural, many people see improvements in sleep, digestion, and overall energy levels.

Spiritual Integration: For spiritually advanced seekers, witnessing closes the gap between spiritual knowledge and everyday experience. Your understanding of ideas like presence, acceptance, and non-attachment becomes embodied rather than just intellectual.

This chapter has given you the foundational tools for developing emotional witnessing—the first and most important step in the WEATHER Method. The 5-second pause, body-scanning techniques, and natural check-in practices offer immediate ways to create space between emotional triggers and automatic reactions. Remember that witnessing isn't about becoming emotionally perfect or reaching some detached spiritual state. It's about developing the ability to stay present with whatever emotional weather arises, knowing that presence creates space for natural emotional movement and healing.

CHAPTER 5: E - EXPLORE THE LANDSCAPE

What if your most difficult emotions were actually sophisticated messengers carrying wisdom? This revelation changes everything about how you approach emotional overwhelm, shifting you from being a victim of your feelings to being a curious explorer of your inner world. When you learn to investigate rather than escape, you discover that every emotion has valuable information about your true needs, values, and growth opportunities.

Many spiritually experienced people try to transcend their emotions too quickly. Maybe you've done this yourself—feeling anger or sadness and immediately reaching for meditation, breathing exercises, or positive affirmations, hoping to make those feelings go away. While this is well-intentioned, it often misses the deeper lessons your emotions are trying to teach.

The exploration phase shifts your relationship with emotions from avoidance to understanding.

Shifting from Elimination to Investigation

. . .

It's natural to want to get rid of difficult emotions. Our brains are wired to avoid pain and chase after pleasure—so of course we want the bad feelings to stop. However, when you apply this survival instinct to your emotions, it can hinder growth and understanding. Instead, if you explore your feelings instead of fighting them, anxiety can become a guide instead of an enemy.

Shifting from trying to rid yourself of feelings to being curious about them is a game-changer. This means approaching your emotions with the same curiosity you'd bring to a good mystery or a tricky puzzle. You're not trying to change anything right away—you're simply interested in understanding what's happening inside you.

Instead of asking, "How do I get rid of this feeling?" you learn to ask, "What is this feeling trying to tell me?"

This simple change in attitude opens entirely new possibilities for understanding and working with your emotions. You're not bypassing your emotions or pretending they don't matter. Instead, you're just observing them, understanding that emotions are part of the natural flow of consciousness.

The Art of Friendly Investigation

Exploring your emotions involves developing specific skills to connect with your inner experience. Instead of thinking of feelings as problems to fix, try seeing them as interesting experiences that deserve your attention and respect.

Quality Questioning

To gather clues, we need to pose provocative questions. Instead of the usual, "Why am I feeling this way?" which often causes overthinking, you'll learn to ask more productive questions:

"What is this emotion telling me?" This approach acknowledges that emotions carry insight deserving of our utmost attention.

"Where do I feel this emotion in my body?" Emotions aren't just thoughts—they show up as physical sensations, too. Maybe anxiety feels like tightness in your chest, excitement as a buzz in your arms, or sadness as heaviness in your stomach. When you notice where emotions show up, you stay grounded in the present moment—instead of getting swept up in stories about your feelings.

"What does this emotion remind me of?" Sometimes, current feelings relate to past experiences or similar patterns. This awareness can give you proper context without the need to "figure out" your emotional patterns intellectually.

"If this emotion could speak, what would it say?" This question prompts your intuitive wisdom instead of your analytical mind. You might be surprised by what comes up when you give your emotions a voice. Often, they have very practical requests: "I need more rest," "I want to feel valued," "I'm excited about this new possibility," or "I'm concerned about this decision."

These questions are designed to encourage your subconscious mind to come forward. There's no need to overthink or try to find the perfect answers—trust that your subconscious will reveal what it needs to when it's ready. Remember, this isn't about getting everything right. It's about exploring your inner world with curiosity and openness.

Understanding Emotional Messages

Every emotion arises from something—a thought, a memory, a physical sensation, an external circumstance, or a combination of factors. Learning to decode these messages provides tremendous insight into your emotional patterns and your appropriate responses to life situations.

External vs. Internal Triggers

External triggers are easier to identify because they are obvious: Your colleague makes a sarcastic remark, and you feel irritated. You receive an unexpected bill, and anxiety arises. Your partner surprises you with flowers, and joy bubbles up. These cause-and-effect links are simple to understand.

Internal triggers require a more subtle level of awareness. For example, you might wake up feeling heavy for no clear reason, only to realize you've been worrying about your mother's health. Or, you could notice irritation during meditation and understand that you're judging yourself for having a "busy mind" again. These internal triggers often reveal your deepest concerns and self-judgments.

Common Emotional Messages

Different emotions usually convey specific kinds of information.

Anger often signals that a key boundary has been crossed or something important to you is at risk. Instead of seeing anger as negative, consider it a helpful warning about what truly matters and what needs to be protected or changed.

Sadness often indicates the loss of something meaningful, unmet needs, or the end of an important relationship. Instead of rushing to feel better, you can use sadness as a guide to understand what needs grieving and what new direction might be calling you.

Fear frequently indicates possible challenges or unknown areas that need careful thought and attention. Instead of viewing fear as a weakness, see it as your system's way of encouraging careful planning or cautious behavior.

Joy shines when your actions mirror your core values. It shows that your decisions and behaviors are true to who you are.

Excitement reveals opportunities that motivate you and align with your natural talents and interests.

Frustration often indicates unresolved tension and might call for a new approach or better communication.

Working with Workplace Emotional Patterns

Professional environments serve as valuable testing grounds for emotional understanding. Your workplace emotions provide important insights into career alignment, workplace relationships, and personal boundaries that can inform both your quick reactions and your overall career decisions.

The Monday Morning Email Storm:

Scenario: You arrived at work to find many urgent emails waiting for you. Your boss asked to meet right away about the project you thought was going well.

Exploring Process:

• Witness: "I am getting anxious, and my breathing is becoming shallow."

• Explore: "This anxiety shows that I need a better way to manage my emails, and I need to have better communication."

• Body Check: Tension in shoulders, rapid heartbeat, shallow breathing.

• Emotional message: "I need a better way to manage competing priorities."

• Meaning: Your anxiety isn't just about the emails; it indicates a need to set better boundaries, priorities, and, most importantly, improve communication with your supervisor.

Performance Review Feedback:

Scenario: Your manager points out problems with how you manage projects during your annual review.

Exploration Process:

• Initial Response: Defensive anger, hurt about your competency being questioned, and slight excitement about potential improvement.

• Message Decoding:

• Anger signals: "My approach should not be brushed aside."

• Hurt reveals: "I care about my work, and I want recognition for my efforts.

• Excitement: "I am willing to grow and learn new things."

• Meaning: Your mixed feelings reveal that you can defend yourself while remaining open to change. This insight is useful for figuring out how to respond effectively.

Relationship Exploration Patterns

Some of the strongest and most intense emotions bubble to the surface when we're interacting with others. Trying to analyze these patterns with curiosity rather than judgment will lead to helpful clues about your needs, boundaries, and ways of communicating.

When Your Partner Triggers Defensiveness

Exploration Questions:

• What am I feeling threatened about now?

• What do I need to feel secure?

• Is this about their tone, or about my need to feel respected?

• What old wound could this be touching?

Often, people realize that the words provoking anger or hurt are not the actual problem. Instead, it's the need to feel heard, valued, or understood. This insight shifts the conversation from defensiveness to genuine, honest communication.

When Your Teenager Dismisses Your Advice

Exploration process:

• Surface emotion: Hurt, frustration, possibly anger.

• Deeper investigation: What does their eye roll mean? What am I really worried about?

• Body awareness: Tightness in the chest and a feeling of deflation.

• Underlying message: "I love them and want to stay connected even as they become independent."

This shows that hurt feelings are not about being right but about maintaining a loving connection with the growing child.

Family Gathering Tensions

Scenario: A family holiday where unspoken tensions make conversations uncomfortable.

Exploration process:

• Environmental awareness: What emotional weather is present in the room?

• Personal response: How is this family interaction affecting my emotional state?

• Value exploration: What is the most important thing to me in family relationships?

• Boundary investigation: How can I get involved without taking on family dysfunction?

. . .

Moving from Analysis to Understanding

The key difference between analysis and exploration is the way you approach the issue. Analysis tries to figure things out mentally, often creating detailed stories about why you feel the way you do. Exploration observes what is happening with objective curiosity.

Analysis asks: "Why do I always react this way? What's wrong with me? How can I fix this pattern?" These questions often lead to self-judgment and mental loops that cause anxiety and cloud judgment.

Exploration asks: "What's here right now? What does this feeling need? How can I respond with wisdom?" These questions create space for understanding to develop naturally without forcing premature solutions.

When you notice yourself overthinking your emotions, gently redirect your focus to direct experience. Feel the physical sensations in your body. Pay attention to your breathing. Observe the emotion itself instead of your thoughts about it. This shift from mental activity to present-moment awareness naturally helps you move toward acceptance—the next step in the WEATHER method.

Practical Exploration in Daily Life

The exploration phase works best when it is smoothly integrated into your daily activities, rather than being a separate practice. You can explore emotions while:

- Drinking your morning coffee

- Walking to work
- Washing dishes
- Waiting in lines
- Taking breaks throughout the day
- Getting ready for bed

This shows that spiritual awakening can occur right in the midst of everyday life. You don't need special conditions or dedicated meditation time to develop emotionally—just a little consistency and curiosity as you go about your day.

The 2-Minute Coffee Exploration

During your morning coffee, you can practice emotional exploration by asking:

- What kind of emotional weather am I feeling right now? (30 seconds of gentle noticing)
- What could have influenced this feeling? (30 seconds of curious investigation)
- What does this emotion indicate I need to do today? (30 seconds of listening for wisdom)
- How can I acknowledge this feeling while continuing with my day? (30 seconds of gentle planning)

This quick exercise helps to develop emotional intelligence without needing extra time or special conditions.

Signs of Skillful Exploration

. . .

You'll recognize you're improving in emotional exploration when:

• You feel genuinely curious about difficult emotions, rather than just wanting to run from them.

• You can recognize emotions and their messages more quickly and accurately.

• You notice your automatic stories about feelings without being controlled by them.

• Emotions feel less overwhelming because you understand how they communicate their messages.

• You use less energy resisting your feelings and more energy gaining insight from them.

• Your emotional vocabulary grows beyond just "good" and "bad" feelings.

• You rely on your emotional intelligence to guide wise responses.

Common Exploration Errors

• Curiosity turns into analysis—when exploration shifts from experience to intellect. You begin overthinking emotions instead of truly feeling them, creating mental stories rather than gaining practical wisdom. If you notice this pattern, return to simple body awareness and being present in the moment.

• Emotional detective work that involves continuously examining past experiences that might relate to current feelings. While some background history can be helpful, avoid getting caught up in emotional archaeology. Stay focused on what the emotion is asking of you in the present.

- Perfectionistic exploration that sees emotional investigation as just another spiritual skill to master perfectly. Remember that exploration should be natural and curious, not forced or fake. If it starts to feel like work, return to simple witnessing until curiosity naturally reappears.

As you become more comfortable exploring your emotions, it naturally gets easier to reach acceptance—the next step in the WEATHER method. When you truly understand what your feelings are asking for, accepting them becomes simpler because you see their purpose. Instead of fighting against overwhelming, random emotions, you start to see them as wise messengers that aim to help you respond better to life's challenges.

CHAPTER 6: A - ACCEPT THE WEATHER

What if the emotions you struggle with the most are actually your greatest teachers? Ancient traditions observed something many of us overlook—acceptance isn't about giving up. It's a gentle yet powerful force for real change. When you stop fighting your emotional weather and start embracing it, those feelings often begin to shift naturally.

This truth challenges everything you've learned about emotional management. Instead of trying to fix, change, or improve your emotional state, acceptance encourages you to meet whatever arises with the same natural ease you'd show to a friend at your door.

Once you genuinely accept what's here, you open the door for natural movement and change to occur.

The Revolutionary Practice of Unconditional Welcome

Most spiritual advice treats tough emotions like unwelcome houseguests—something you just tolerate until they finally leave.

But what if these feelings aren't interruptions to your spiritual practice? What if they are your spiritual practice?

At the core of emotional acceptance is the concept of unconditional welcome. It involves showing every emotion with the same openness, regardless of how intense it is, how long it lasts, or how "acceptable" it appears. You don't need to understand your emotions or judge if they're spiritual enough—simply let them in because they are present.

When anger flares up, your first thought is probably, "How do I get rid of this?" When sadness sits heavy in your chest, you begin planning its departure. And when anxiety appears, you immediately look for ways to make it stop. It's easy to treat emotions like problems to fix rather than recognizing them as natural weather patterns passing through the sky of your awareness.

Essential Acceptance Phrases That Transform Your Inner Weather

The language you use internally influences how likely you are to work with your emotions. These phrases help you move from being resistant to being open:

For Difficult Emotions:

- "This anger is welcome here."

- "I make space for this sadness."

- "This anxiety belongs here, too."

- "I accept what I'm feeling right now."

- "This frustration is allowed to be here."

For Overwhelming Emotions:

- "I don't need to fix this feeling."
- "This intensity is temporary weather."
- "I can hold space for this without drowning."
- "This emotion is moving through me, not defining me."

For Resistance to Emotions:

- "My resistance is also welcome here."
- "I accept that I can't accept this right now."
- "This struggle is part of my human experience."
- "I'm learning to be with what is."

What makes these phrases powerful is that they don't have an agenda—no magic tricks, no forcing feelings away. You're not trying to rush your emotions out the door or prove how spiritual you are. You're simply working with what's already here because fighting your feelings is a battle you'll never win.

Workplace Acceptance Applications

In professional settings, we often encounter situations that trigger challenging emotions. The important part is learning to accept these feelings and respond to workplace stress with calmness and understanding, rather than letting them take over or reacting unprofessionally.

Accepting Performance Anxiety

Scenario: You're about to deliver a presentation to senior leadership, and anxiety rushes through you.

Old pattern: Struggling with anxiety, telling yourself you shouldn't feel nervous, trying to force calm confidence.

Acceptance approach:

- "This anxiety is welcome here—it shows I care about doing well."

- "My nervous system is preparing me for an important moment."

- "I can feel anxious and still deliver an effective presentation."

- "This energy can actually enhance my focus and engagement."

Professional benefit: When you accept anxiety instead of fighting it, you put your energy into preparation—rather than wrestling with yourself. That anxiety can actually turn into helpful focus and alertness.

Accepting Criticism and Feedback

Scenario: Your manager gave blunt feedback about your project in front of colleagues.

Acceptance practice:

- Witness: "I notice hurt and anger arising from public criticism."

- Accept: "These feelings are completely understandable and welcome."

- Respond: "Thank you for the feedback. Can we schedule time to discuss specific improvements?"

Key insight: Recognizing your emotions in response to criticism doesn't imply that you must tolerate unfair treatment. You can acknowledge your feelings while maintaining a professional demeanor.

Accepting Workplace Conflict

Scenario: Two colleagues argued during a team meeting, creating tension for everyone.

Acceptance process:

- Personal weather: "I notice anxiety about conflict and the urge to either fix this or escape."

- Welcome response: "This discomfort is natural—almost everyone feels tense during conflict."

- Professional application: "I can accept my discomfort without taking sides or trying to manage their emotions."

Accepting your feelings helps you stay effective at work—without getting swept up in the drama.

Releasing the Compulsion to Fix Your Emotional State

The spiritual marketplace has conditioned you to believe that every uncomfortable emotion signals a problem that needs immediate attention.

Always trying to fix yourself sends a quiet but powerful message—your natural emotional responses aren't okay as they are. You end up feeling like you need to be managed or improved. But what if that urge to change your feelings is actually blocking the freedom you're searching for?

Every emotion arises for a reason. If you rush to change how you feel, you'll completely overlook the valuable messages those feelings can convey.

The practice of releasing the fixing compulsion begins with patience.

When you pause and listen, you'd discover that emotions have their own intelligence and timing, and they often resolve themselves more efficiently when given space rather than interference.

Understanding Emotions as Temporary Visitors

Knowing that no emotion lasts forever is liberating. But when we're caught up in intense feelings, it can feel like it's our new permanent state! When anxiety takes over, it seems like peace will never return. It's important to remember that change is inevitable—this is a universal truth.

Emotions are like weather systems moving through the sky of your mind. A thunderstorm never becomes the sky itself—no matter how intense it gets. The storm rolls in, does its thing, and eventually passes, leaving the sky unchanged. The same is true for your strongest emotions—they're just passing through the steady awareness that is always you.

The Guest House Practice

Imagine emotions are guests in your house. Some are like dear friends, others are like messy strangers. The practice of emotional hospitality involves welcoming all emotions with the same basic courtesy and hospitality you'd show to any guests turning up at your house. You don't need to love difficult emotions, but you can acknowledge them without the urge to suppress or ignore them.

When challenging emotions arrive at your inner guest house:

- Open the door - Notice the emotion without hiding or pretending it isn't there.

- Offer a warm welcome - Use one of your acceptance phrases: "Anger, you're welcome here."

- Provide space - Let the emotion be, without trying to soothe or entertain it.

- Trust that the visit has a purpose - Remember that all emotions carry information or energy that serves you.

- Allow natural departure - Don't hurry to send the visitor away, but also don't beg them to stay.

This practice is effective because it aligns with the natural flow of emotional energy. When you accept emotions, they can move on naturally without getting trapped in the system, as would be the case if you resist them.

When Acceptance Feels Impossible

Some emotional states feel so intense or uncomfortable that acceptance seems completely unreasonable.

If you're feeling overwhelmed by grief and complete acceptance seems out of reach, you could start by accepting your current inability to accept: "I notice I can't welcome this grief right now, and my resistance is understandable." This helps prevent you from adding rejection to your grief, which only makes suffering worse.

Sometimes acceptance occurs in layers:

- First layer: Accepting that the emotion is present, even if you don't like it.

- Second layer: Accepting the intensity of the feeling without needing to change it.

- Third layer: Welcoming the emotion as part of your human experience.

- Fourth layer: Finding gratitude for the information conveyed by the emotion.

You don't need to reach all layers right away. Even accepting that you can't accept is a step toward emotional freedom.

Emergency Acceptance Protocols

. . .

When emotions feel too overwhelming for acceptance

• Lower your standards - aim for 10% less resistance rather than full acceptance.

• Focus on breathing - sometimes, simply being aware of your breath is good enough.

• Use your body - feel your feet on the ground or your back against a chair.

• Remember impermanence - this emotional weather will shift, even if it does so gradually.

• Seek appropriate support - sometimes professional help is needed.

When you feel emotionally numb

• Numbness is also a valid emotional weather that deserves acceptance.

• Don't force feelings—just observe their absence with curiosity.

• Numbness often precedes natural emotional movement.

• Practice gentle self-compassion rather than judgment.

True acceptance instantly brings a sense of spaciousness around emotional experiences. When you stop resisting your feelings, you realize there is plenty of room in your awareness for whatever comes up. This space isn't something you have to force into existence—it's what naturally appears when resistance fades.

Consider the physical sensations of acceptance versus resistance. When you resist an emotion, your body often tightens. Your shoulders might tense up, your breathing can become shallow, and your jaw may clench. These physical responses create a feeling of tightness and pressure that can feel worse than the original emotion.

When you truly accept what's happening, your body naturally starts to soften. Your breathing becomes deeper, your muscles relax, and a feeling of spaciousness surrounds the sensation. This isn't a technique you apply—it's what happens automatically when you stop resisting your experience.

Practical Daily Applications

Incorporating acceptance into daily life requires specific practices that help you remember and use these principles when emotions come up. The key is becoming familiar with acceptance during calm moments so it can be accessible during emotional intensity.

The STOP Practice

This simple framework helps you apply acceptance in real-time:

• Stop whatever you're doing when you notice emotional intensity.

• Take a conscious breath to create a moment of space.

• Observe the emotion present without rushing to change it.

• Proceed with whatever response seems appropriate after offering acceptance.

This practice can be applied to micro-emotions that arise throughout the day—the slight irritation when technology misbehaves, the brief disappointment when plans change, the flash of anxiety before a difficult conversation. By practicing acceptance with minor emotions, you develop the ability to handle stronger feelings when they come up.

Daily Acceptance Integration

. . .

Morning Acceptance Intention: Begin each day with the goal of accepting whatever emotional weather shows up. This doesn't mean looking for difficult emotions, but being receptive to whatever arises with curiosity instead of resistance.

Acceptance Check-ins: Several times throughout the day, pause and ask, "What am I feeling right now, and can I welcome it?" Notice any resistance and extend acceptance to it as well.

Evening Acceptance Review: Before going to sleep, think about times when you successfully embraced difficult emotions and moments when you struggled to accept them. Use this insight to improve your practice.

Beyond Personal Acceptance: Accepting Others' Weather

When you become comfortable with your own emotional state, you'll become more accepting of others' feelings. This results in meaningful improvements in your relationships, as people feel more comfortable being around you.

Accepting others' emotions doesn't mean:

• Taking on their emotional states as your own.

• Agreeing with their actions or decisions.

• Remaining in damaging circumstances.

• Ignoring your boundaries or needs.

Accepting others' emotions does mean:

• Allowing them to experience feelings without attempting to fix or change them.

- Staying present without getting overwhelmed.
- Responding with wisdom instead of reaction.
- Trusting their ability to manage their own emotional weather.

Workplace Applications of Accepting Others

When a colleague is stressed, instead of trying to immediately cheer them up or fix their problems, offer your presence: "I can see you're having a tough day. Is there anything specific I can help with, or would you prefer some space?"

When conflicts arise within the team, let's focus on staying calm and open. We can say, "I see there are some strong feelings here. Let's make sure everyone gets a chance to share before we decide how to move ahead."

When dealing with difficult clients, recognize that their frustration or anger reflects their emotional state at the moment without taking it personally: "I understand you're upset about this situation. Let's concentrate on finding a solution that is effective for you."

Troubleshooting Acceptance Challenges

Even with a clear understanding and genuine practice, you'll face situations where acceptance seems hard or impossible. These challenges are normal parts of developing emotional mastery.

When you are unable to accept the emotion

When emotions feel overwhelming, remember that acceptance doesn't mean you have to contain or control the feeling. You're simply choosing to stop fighting what's already there. The emotion isn't too big for acceptance—your resistance is making it seem larger than it truly is.

Try this approach:

• Recognize the magnitude: "This grief feels overwhelming"

• Release control: "I can't contain this, and I don't need to."

• Offer space: "I make space for this enormous feeling."

• Trust the process: "This emotion knows how to move through me."

When accepting this emotion feels like giving up

Acceptance isn't passive resignation—it's active engagement with reality. When you accept an emotion, you're not agreeing that the situation causing it should continue. You're simply acknowledging it so that you can make an informed decision instead of reacting impulsively.

Remember:

• Accepting anger doesn't mean putting up with abuse.

• Accepting sadness doesn't mean remaining in harmful situations.

• Accepting fear doesn't mean avoiding necessary action.

• Accepting joy doesn't mean getting too attached to good experiences.

When you keep forgetting to practice acceptance

Developing new emotional habits takes time and patience. Most people forget to practice acceptance until it's too late. This is completely normal.

Helpful strategies:

- Use daily routines as reminders to practice acceptance (such as every time you drink water).

- Place visual cues for reminders, such as a small stone on your desk or a note on your mirror.

- Practice with smaller emotions to develop the habit before major storms come.

- Be kind to yourself if you forget—honesty and self-compassion are just other ways of practicing acceptance.

The revolutionary shift from resistance to acceptance transforms your entire relationship with emotional experience. What once felt like enemies become teachers. What once caused suffering becomes insight. What once seemed permanent reveals itself as fleeting weather passing through the vast sky of your being.

As you get ready for the next step in the WEATHER method—learning how to go with the natural ups and downs of your emotions—you're building on this solid foundation of accepting whatever comes. Welcoming your feelings as they are is what lets you see how they move and change on their own, as long as you give them a little breathing room.

CHAPTER 7: T - TRANSITION WITH FLOW

When you stop fighting your feelings, they tend to pass on their own. It's kind of like trying to make a river go uphill—you just can't do it, and forcing it only makes things worse. The ancient Taoists understood this well: by going with the flow of life instead of battling against it, we can handle our emotions more smoothly and gracefully.

Understanding Natural Emotional Rhythms

Your emotions follow natural rhythms similar to the seasons. Just as seasons change, emotions cycle through rising, peaking, and calming phases. Recognizing these patterns can make it easier to manage and understand your feelings.

Think about how storms move across the sky. They don't ask for permission or apologize for their strength. They just show up, do their thing, and then leave. Your emotions work the same way—there's a natural intelligence in how they come and go.

. . .

Emotional Timing Patterns

Each emotion has its natural rhythm and duration. Here's what you can expect from different emotional weather patterns:

Anger burns hot and fast—if you let it move through you, it usually passes in minutes.

Sadness flows like rain—sometimes it's a gentle drizzle, sometimes a heavy downpour, but it always has its own rhythm and breaks.

Anxiety moves like wind—restless and always changing, and it often settles down when you stop trying to force it away.

Fear strikes like lightning—sharp and quick when there's real danger, but it can linger when you're facing imagined threats.

Joy radiates like sunshine—spreads naturally when you let it, and shines brightest when you don't try to hold on too tight.

Trusting the natural timing of emotions means letting them run their course—without rushing to fix them or dragging them out longer than they need to last.

The Futility of Emotional Force

Most of us treat tough emotions like we're in a boxing ring with a heavyweight champion—throwing punches, hoping to knock out our sadness or anxiety before they hit us. But emotions aren't enemies to defeat—they're waves of energy that want to pass through you and maybe even teach you something along the way.

When you try to force an emotion to pass quickly, you're essentially telling your nervous system that its natural intelligence is wrong. When you feel inner conflict, your body reacts by creating more tension and resistance. This reaction results in experiencing even more of the emotion you want to avoid.

Workplace Example: Consider Marcus, a project manager who takes pride in staying calm under pressure. When his team missed a critical deadline due to factors beyond his control, waves of frustration and anxiety overwhelmed his professional composure. Instead of letting these natural responses flow, he immediately started using breathing techniques, positive affirmations, and attempts to "think rationally" about the situation.

For hours, Marcus wrestled with his emotions, growing more desperate. The harder he tried to rise above his frustration, the more agitated he became. The more he fought his anxiety, the heavier it felt. He was trapped in a draining cycle of emotional struggle—a battle he couldn't win because he was fighting against his own natural processing system.

The truth is that emotions follow their own timeline, and your role isn't to control that schedule.

Learning to Ride Emotional Waves

The metaphor of surfing perfectly illustrates the art of emotional transition. Surfers don't try to control the wave—they learn to understand how the wave breaks, position themselves in the right spot, get on the wave just before it breaks, and ride it in harmony with the wave's energy. Emotional mastery works similarly.

When Marcus finally understood the wave metaphor, he decided to test it during his next workplace crisis. During a budget meeting where unexpected cuts were announced, he felt the familiar rush of anger and worry building inside him. Instead of fighting the emotional wave, he thought to himself, "Here comes a strong wave. Let me see where it wants to take me."

Morning Coffee

He noticed that the anger provided him with clear information—it indicated the team's real need for resources and his role to advocate for them. Instead of trying to suppress the anger, he allowed it to reveal what action was necessary. The wave naturally guided him toward a conversation with senior leadership about alternative solutions.

To his surprise, the anger didn't consume his day as it usually did. By working with its natural flow instead of fighting against it, the emotion served its purpose and gradually dissolved within an hour. The wave had carried him exactly where he needed to go.

The Anatomy of an Emotional Wave

Every emotional wave follows a predictable pattern that you can learn to navigate.

• The Swell—The initial surge of emotional energy, often experienced as physical sensations before conscious awareness.

• The Build—Growing intensity as the emotion intensifies and approaches peak expression.

• The Crest—The peak of intensity where emotion demands acknowledgment and often delivers its clearest message.

• The Break—The sudden release of emotional energy when resistance is removed.

• The Wash—The gradual return to emotional equilibrium, accompanied by clarity and insight.

This analogy helps you understand where to position yourself at each stage. In the swell, you observe and prepare. During the build, you explore with curiosity. At the crest, you accept. At the break, you allow expression to flow naturally. In the wash, you harmonize the wisdom gained.

Working with Different Emotional Weather Patterns

Just as you dress differently for rain than for snow, different emotional weather patterns call for different approaches during the transition phase.

Navigating Anger Storms

Anger is quick, intense energy that seeks to bring about change. When anger surfaces:

• Feel the heat without rushing to act—anger's message is usually about boundaries.

• Let it burn clean through your system without giving it extra mental fuel about how wrong others are.

• Use your energy for constructive actions once the initial surge has passed. Anger usually subsides quickly if you don't resist feeling it or acting on its urges immediately. The emotion aims to restore balance, not cause destruction.

Workplace Application: When your colleague takes credit for your work during a presentation, the anger that arises offers valuable insights into boundaries and fair treatment. Instead of immediately confronting them or suppressing the feeling, let the anger guide you to what needs to be addressed. The emotional energy can support a clear, professional conversation about attribution and teamwork.

Flowing with Sadness

Sadness is like gentle rain—it aims to cleanse and nourish rather than destroy. When sadness appears:

• Allow the flow without rushing to feel improved or cheer yourself up.

• Honor what is being mourned—sadness often signifies the end of something precious.

• Trust the timing—sadness follows its rhythm and cannot be rushed.

Sadness often arrives in waves over time, rather than resolving in a single session. Each wave typically removes another layer of what needs to be released.

Professional Example: When Lisa's favorite coworker announced they were leaving the company, a wave of sadness washed over her. Instead of quickly focusing on the positive side, like new opportunities, she took the time to mourn the end of their daily conversations and the friendship that was lost. By recognizing her feelings, she was able to handle the loss naturally, which gave her sincere support during this change.

Dancing with Anxiety

Anxiety is restless energy that frequently indicates uncertainty or a need for preparation. When anxiety moves through:

• Ground yourself physically—feel your feet, notice your breathing, and connect with your body.

• Distinguish real concerns from imagined ones—anxiety often blurs the line between legitimate preparation and unfounded fears.

• Channel the energy—anxiety's restlessness often subsides through proper action or movement.

Anxiety often shifts when you either address its practical concerns or let its energy be released through gentle movement.

Workplace Strategy: Before important presentations, instead of trying to eliminate nervousness, use the anxious energy to focus on final preparations. That restlessness can motivate a thorough review of materials, practicing key points, and mentally rehearsing potential questions.

Welcoming Fear

Fear is your body's way of trying to keep you safe, though it sometimes overreacts to threats that aren't physical. When fear shows up:

• Assess real danger versus perceived threat—most modern fears don't trigger fight-or-flight responses.

• Breathe into your body—fear often tightens breathing and causes physical tension.

• Move toward what you're avoiding when appropriate—fear often fades away through gentle, mindful action.

Fear shifts rapidly when confronting real dangers or gradually when dealing with growth challenges.

The Three Skills of Emotional Transition

Skill One: Reading the Emotional Forecast

Just as meteorologists can forecast weather patterns, you can learn to interpret your emotional climate. This involves becoming attuned to the subtle changes that signal upcoming emotional storms. Your body constantly provides clues about upcoming emotional shifts if you know how to listen.

Physical tension often comes before emotional shifts. For example, you might notice your shoulders tightening, your jaw clenching, or your breathing becoming shallow. These are early warning signs of emotional buildup. Instead of ignoring these signals, become aware of them and use them to prepare yourself.

Energy levels are a reliable sign. You might suddenly feel exhausted, unusually restless, or mysteriously on edge without any clear external reason. Your energetic system often detects emotional shifts first, sometimes hours before you're consciously aware of them.

Professional Application: Notice if specific types of meetings regularly drain your energy or if certain colleagues trigger subtle tension in your body. This awareness helps you manage your emotions and establish healthy boundaries.

Skill Two: Positioning for Natural Flow

After you've recognized the incoming emotional weather, the next skill is to position yourself to work with its natural movement instead of fighting it. This means creating the right conditions for emotions to flow through you smoothly without getting stuck or causing unnecessary drama.

Your physical posture is more important than many realize. Emotions are partly physical, and your body position can influence their natural flow. When difficult emotions come up, avoid collapsing inward or tensing up. Instead, maintain an open and relaxed posture that allows energy to move smoothly through your system.

Mentally, adopt a curious and neutral stance rather than one of resistance or attachment. Think of this from the perspective of a scientist observing a fascinating event in nature. The scientist does not try to alter what is happening. Instead, they observe and gather data on how the emotional system functions.

Skill Three: Trusting the Natural Resolution

The most challenging skill for most people is learning to trust that emotions will naturally resolve on their own without forcing them. Your emotional system has been effectively processing experiences since birth—it knows how to complete its cycles if you don't interfere with its natural flow.

This trust develops gradually through direct experience. Each time you allow an emotion to follow its natural course without forcing early resolution, you enhance your confidence in your system's ability to self-regulate. Like learning to float in water, the more you relax and trust, the more naturally buoyant you become.

Creating Space for Natural Movement

Emotions need room to move, just like water needs a clear channel to flow freely. This space isn't physical—it's the psychological openness that comes from not instantly reacting to or trying to fix your emotional experience.

When you feel angry, instead of reacting impulsively or suppressing it, try taking a deep breath. This creates space without dismissing the anger, letting it pass peacefully without causing unnecessary harm to yourself or others.

When sadness arises, instead of rushing to distract yourself or forcing positivity, create space by allowing the sadness to exist without trying to immediately change it. This space lets the emotion go through its natural cycle of expression and resolution.

The Practice of Emotional Spaciousness

- Pause before reacting to any emotional intensity—just five seconds can create significant space.

- Breathe intentionally when emotions surface—breath creates literal space in your body for feeling.

- Relax your body—tension blocks emotional flow, while relaxation encourages it to flow.

- Drop mental commentary—stories about emotions can hinder their natural flow.

Working with Emotional Resistance

The biggest obstacle to natural emotional flow is the resistance your mind creates when you try to control the timing of your emotions. This resistance shows up as internal commentary about your emotions—judging them as wrong, trying to figure out why they're happening, or creating stories about what they mean about you as a person.

This mental layer has nothing to do with the emotion itself. It's like adding a layer of concrete over a natural stream—the water wants to flow, but the artificial barrier causes it to back up and stagnate. When you remove the mental resistance, emotions flow naturally without creating psychological buildup.

The practice involves connecting directly with the physical sensation of the emotion itself, the moment you realize you're adding commentary to the emotion. Instead of thinking about your anger, feel the heat in your chest. Instead of analyzing your sadness, notice the heaviness in your heart.

Signs of Natural Emotional Resolution

Learning to recognize when emotions are naturally resolving helps you avoid trying to force completion when the process is already happening organically. Natural resolution has distinct characteristics that differ from forced suppression or distraction.

When emotions resolve naturally, you'll notice a gradual decrease in intensity rather than a sudden disappearance. The feeling doesn't vanish—it softens and shifts into something more manageable. You might still detect traces of the original emotion, but without the urgent charge that demanded immediate attention.

Your breathing naturally deepens as emotional storms pass. Your shoulders relax, your jaw loosens, and your overall energy shifts from tightness to openness. These physical changes indicate that your nervous system is returning to normal without force.

Mental clarity arises naturally as emotions settle down. Instead of obsessing over the trigger, you can think clearly about appropriate responses. This clarity often reveals what the emotion was trying to communicate or what action might be needed.

Practical Daily Applications

. . .

The transition skill is most useful during everyday emotional ups and downs rather than only during major crises. Developing this ability during normal emotional fluctuations prepares you for bigger challenges.

Morning Transition Practice

Begin each day by observing your emotional state without attempting to change it. If you wake up feeling anxious about upcoming tasks, allow the anxiety to be present while you enjoy your coffee. Notice where it shows up in your body, think about what it might be telling you about your day, and let it move naturally as you get ready for your activities.

Workday Emotional Flow

Use natural transitions during your workday—like walking between meetings, checking emails, or taking breaks—as opportunities to check in with your emotional state and release any built-up tension naturally.

Evening Emotional Clearing

Before sleep, take a few moments to let any emotional residue from the day fade naturally. This isn't about forcing relaxation, but about creating space for emotions to process before resting.

Moving Beyond Emotional Management

The goal of emotional transition isn't to become someone who never feels difficult emotions—it's to become someone who can experience any emotion without losing their center or wisdom. This represents a fundamental shift from emotional management to emotional mastery.

The emotional management view sees emotions as issues to fix. Emotional mastery recognizes that emotions are natural parts of a healthy mind that can be guided instead of suppressed or resisted. This shift in perspective changes how you relate to emotional patterns.

When you stop trying to control your emotions and instead learn to dance with them, you realize that your emotional system is surprisingly intelligent and self-regulating. The storms that once felt overwhelming become opportunities to practice presence. The difficult feelings that once ruined your day turn into insights that guide wiser decisions.

This mastery isn't about becoming emotionally numb or spiritually superior—it's about developing the natural ability to feel everything fully while maintaining your essential stability and wisdom. You become like a mountain that endures all weather without being fundamentally disturbed by any of it.

As you develop skill with emotional transition and learn to trust the natural timing of your inner weather patterns, you'll discover that working with emotions rather than against them opens space for the next phase of the WEATHER method. In the following chapter, we'll explore how to transform emotional experiences into practical wisdom by aligning your insights with conscious responses that honor both your emotional intelligence and your life circumstances.

CHAPTER 8: H - HARMONIZE WISDOM WITH RESPONSE

Your emotions aren't just random storms—they're wise messengers, each offering guidance for living authentically. Once you learn to notice, explore, accept, and move through your emotional weather, you're ready for the next big step: how do you turn this understanding into action? This stage involves transforming emotional awareness into practical wisdom, so you can use your inner weather as a trusted guide for all your decisions.

The harmonization step is when spiritual insight turns into practical wisdom.

Deciphering Emotional Messages to Guide Decisions

Every emotion reveals something about your current life circumstances. Instead of asking, "How do I make this feeling go away?" focus on asking, "What is this emotion indicating about what I need or value right now?"

. . .

QUINN PATH

The Emotional Intelligence Decision Framework

When making decisions—from everyday choices to significant events—use this framework to tap into your emotional wisdom.

• Pause and Check Emotional Weather: Before making a decision, take 30 seconds to check your emotional weather.

• Identify the Signal: What specific emotions are associated with each option?

• Decode the Message: What is each emotion trying to tell you?

• Cross-Reference Values: How well do these emotional signals match your core values?

• Choose Wisely: Pick the option that respects both emotional insight and practical needs.

Primary Emotional Signals and Their Messages

Emotion	Typical Message	Decision Guidance
Excitement	"This aligns with my authentic interests."	Move toward with appropriate preparation
Anxiety	"This matters to me, and it needs careful attention."	Gather more information, prepare thoroughly
Anger	"My boundaries or values are being violated."	Address the underlying issue, set clear limits
Sadness	"I'm grieving something valuable that's ending."	Accept the loss while remaining open to new possibilities
Fear	"This involves unknown territory or genuine risk."	Assess realistic dangers, prepare appropriately
Joy	"This serves my highest good and true nature."	Embrace while maintaining balance
Frustration	"My current approach isn't working effectively."	Try a different strategy or seek support.

Workplace Decision-Making with Emotional Intelligence

Work offers many opportunities to combine emotional wisdom with smart decision-making. The feelings you experience at work actually reveal a lot—about your goals, your boundaries, and what you need to grow, both now and later.

Career Transition Decisions

Example: You're offered a promotion that requires relocating to a different city.

Emotional Weather Check: Initial excitement about career advancement, anxiety about leaving current community, sadness about ending current role, fear about unknown challenges.

Decision Framework Application:

• Excitement suggests a career advancement opportunity.

• Anxiety points to practical concerns needing attention (housing, schools, social connections).

• Sadness shows what you value about the current situation.

• Fear indicates a need for more information and preparation.

A harmonized approach means making a plan that honors both your ambitions and your relationships. Let your emotions help you figure out what support and resources you'll need, instead of relying only on logic.

Difficult Colleague Navigation

Example: A team member regularly claims credit for your ideas during presentations.

Emotional Weather: Feelings of anger over unfair treatment, frustration with team dynamics, disappointment due to lack of recognition, and a slight fear of confrontation.

Message Integration:

• Anger signals boundary violation requiring action.

• Frustration indicates a system problem that needs addressing.

• Disappointment reveals your need for acknowledgment.

• Fear suggests a need for a skillful approach.

Response Strategy: Clearly document contributions and address the pattern professionally: "I've noticed that Project X, which we developed together, was presented as primarily your work. Let's discuss how we can ensure both our contributions are acknowledged in future presentations."

Advanced Workplace Applications

Managing Up with Emotional Intelligence

When your boss is under pressure and becomes more demanding, your stress response gives you helpful information. Instead of reacting defensively or getting overwhelmed right away, use your emotional signals to guide your approach.

For example, if you sense your boss's anxiety: "I notice this project has a lot of moving parts. Do you want me to provide daily updates rather than waiting for our weekly check-in?"

Leading Teams Through Emotional Wisdom

If all members of a working group experience difficulty in meeting the deadline, then your anxiety about the project's completion will provide insight into how to assign resources better or communicate.

Anxiety about quality may be addressed in this way: "I want us to deliver our best work. Let's identify which elements are essential and which we can streamline."

If we are concerned about team stress, we could say: "I notice we're all feeling pressure. What support do you need to maintain both quality and well-being?"

Client Relationship Management

When clients become demanding, your emotional reactions help set appropriate boundaries and provide proper service.

We might deal with frustration caused by unrealistic expectations in this way: "I want to make sure that we are aligned on what can be achieved within this timeline and budget. Let's clarify the scope so that everybody is set for success."

Concern for client satisfaction might lead us to this realization: "Your satisfaction is important to us. Help me understand what specific outcome would make this project successful for you."

Advanced Response Strategies by Emotional Pattern

Different emotional weather patterns call for different response strategies. These approaches help you work with your natural emotional style, rather than forcing yourself into one-size-fits-all solutions.

For Quick Emotional Processors

Traits: Experience emotions intensely but briefly, and typically respond quickly; openly communicate their feelings.

Harmonization Strategies:

• Avoid responding too soon: wait 10 seconds instead of 5.

- Verbalise your emotions before engaging in any action: "I'm feeling frustrated about this deadline, and I want to respond constructively."

- Have "cooling off" procedures for critical decisions.

- Release the energy from your feelings through physical activity before engaging in any meaningful conversation.

Workplace Application: If you process emotions quickly, your immediate reactions often give useful first-impression data. Use this skill by sharing your initial response while taking a moment to think more deeply: "My first reaction is concern about this timeline. Let me think through the details and get back to you with specific thoughts."

For Deep Emotional Processors

Traits: Those individuals whose emotions develop slowly, requiring careful thought, and whose feelings must be understood before acting.

Harmonization Strategies:

- Set clear time limits for emotional processing to make informed, final decisions.

- Use writing to clarify emotional messages: "What are my feelings telling me about this situation?"

- Build confidence by resolving minor issues more quickly.

- Create external accountability for moving from processing to action.

Professional Example: If you need time to process feedback before responding, acknowledge this without delaying your response: "Thank you for this feedback. I want to consider it carefully. Could we schedule some time tomorrow to talk about my thoughts and the next steps?"

For Emotional Stackers

Traits: Develops emotions gradually; the person often doesn't realize the buildup until the floodgates open or the pressure becomes overwhelming.

Harmonization Strategies:

• Conduct daily emotional weather check-ins to identify patterns early.

• Practice making decisions when emotional intensity is moderate (not high or low).

• Develop early warning systems: "When I notice X, it usually means Y is building."

• Establish regular "emotional clearing" routines to prevent buildup.

Workplace Strategy: If you tend to accumulate stress over time, develop systems for regular emotional well-being. This includes weekly one-on-ones with your manager to address concerns before they escalate, as well as daily quick check-ins with yourself to evaluate what's working and what needs attention.

For Emotional Avoiders

Traits: Prefers logical analysis over emotional intuition; may find it difficult to grasp emotional information.

Harmonization Strategies:

• Start with body awareness: "What physical sensations accompany this decision?"

• Use emotional vocabulary cards to identify subtle feelings.

• Try the gut check method: "What is my intuition telling me about this?"

- Use an awareness of feelings alongside logical consideration, rather than replacing the latter.

Professional Application: If you usually make decisions using only logic, try adding emotional intelligence: "The data supports Option A, and I also notice I feel more energized when I imagine implementing it. Let me explore what that tells me about sustainability and team engagement."

Practical Decision-Making Tools

The Three-Option Framework

When making difficult decisions, ensure you identify three options to gauge your emotional reaction toward each.

- Option A: Your logical, practical choice
- Option B: Your intuitive, heart-based choice
- Option C: A creative alternative that blends elements of both.

For each option, notice:

- Your immediate emotional response.
- How does your body feel when you imagine choosing this path?
- Feelings of worry or excitement might come to the surface.
- Does this decision align with your values and long-term goals?

Workplace Example: The decision to accept a job offer:

- Option A (Logical): Apply for the position for career development and higher pay.
- Option B (Intuitive): Intuition tells you not to go for a position elsewhere.

- Option C (Creative): Accept with negotiated terms that address concerns about work-life balance and growth opportunities.

The Future Self Check

Picture yourself a year from now, reflecting on this choice:
- Which decision would your future self thank you for making?
- What emotional weather would each path have over time?
- What would you regret not trying?
- Which option would be most true to who you want to be?

The Values Alignment Test

List your top five core values, then rate each decision option (1-10) based on how well it upholds each value.

Example Values Assessment:
- Authenticity: How true am I to myself with this choice?
- Growth: How much will this challenge and develop me?
- Connection: How will this impact my relationships?
- Service: How does this add to the bigger picture?
- Freedom: How much autonomy will this offer?

Troubleshooting Conflicting Emotional Signals

. . .

Sometimes emotions seem to oppose each other, leading to decision paralysis. When handled skillfully, these conflicts often reveal valuable insights.

Excitement vs. Anxiety about the Same Opportunity

- What's happening: Growth opportunities naturally evoke both emotions

- How to harmonize: Explore what specifically excites you versus what worries you.

- Action approach: Tackle the anxiety-producing elements while progressing toward the excitement.

Guilt vs. Relief about Setting Boundaries

- What's happening: Old programming clashes with healthy self-care.

- How to harmonize: Differentiate between helpful guilt (values violation) and inherited guilt (people-pleasing patterns).

- Action approach: Opt for relief when guilt results from unhealthy conditioning.

Anger vs. Sadness about the Same Situation

- What's happening: Complex situations often provoke multiple valid responses.

- How to harmonize: Honor both emotions—anger about injustice and sadness about loss.

- Action approach: Channel anger's energy into productive actions while allowing sadness to be processed naturally.

Joy vs. Fear about Success

- What's happening: Success can cause both appreciation and fear of loss or change.

- How to harmonize: Celebrate achievements while recognizing natural human worries about change.

- Action approach: Enjoy success fully while taking practical steps to maintain what matters most.

Conflict Resolution

When emotional signals seem contradictory:

- Map Each Emotion: Identify every emotion and its specific message.

- Identify the Common Thread: What core need or value links all these feelings?

- Identify the Fear: What do you fear might happen if you embrace each emotion?

- Seek integration: Is there a response that respects the core truth of each feeling?

- Test Timing: Sometimes conflicting emotions suggest you need more time or information.

Real-Time Response Strategies

The STOP-LOOK-CHOOSE Method

For urgent situations that require quick harmonization:

- STOP: Take a 5-second pause to avoid an automatic reaction.

- LOOK: Assess your emotional state - what's happening right now?

- CHOOSE: Pick the response based on emotional wisdom and situational needs.

Emotional Weather Emergency Responses

When overwhelmed by emotional intensity

- First: Ensure safety and basic needs are met.
- Second: Use your breath to make room for wisdom.
- Third: Ask, "What does this intensity need from me right now?"
- Fourth: Take the smallest sensible action.

When emotionally numb or disconnected

- First: Recognize numbness as a valid emotional state.
- Second: Pay attention to body sensations and physical needs.
- Third: Base decisions on values instead of feelings.
- Fourth: Work toward reconnecting with gentle nature, movement, or trusted relationships.

When emotions change rapidly

- First: Recognize the ability to change without judgment.
- Second: Identify underlying patterns or needs behind surface emotions.
- Third: Make decisions based on core values instead of changing feelings.
- Fourth: Communicate your emotional weather to others when appropriate.

. . .

Integration Practices for Daily Harmonization

Morning Intention Setting

Before checking email or starting your daily tasks:

- Know your emotional weather for the day.

- Note any decisions that need attention.

- Set the purpose of aligning feelings with actions.

- If any emotional weather suggests a change of plans, take note.

Midday Decision Checkpoint

During lunch or afternoon break:

- Review all decisions made so far - were they aligned with emotional wisdom?

- Notice what emotional weather has developed since this morning.

- Adjust the afternoon approach based on current emotional information.

- Practice one small decision using the emotional intelligence framework.

Evening Harmonization Review

Before bed:

- Reflect on the choices made during the day.

- Notice where your emotional wisdom guided you well.

- Identify overlooked opportunities for better integration.

- Appreciate efforts to combine feelings with conscious decision-making.

Advanced Harmonization Applications

Creative Projects and Career Decisions

Use emotional weather to inform creative and professional decisions.

• Which projects create lasting excitement compared to fleeting manic energy?

• What work environments align with your natural emotional rhythms?

• How do various career paths influence your fundamental emotional state?

• What creative expressions arise from genuine emotional truth?

Professional Example: Sarah, a marketing director, notices that she feels excited about client projects involving environmental sustainability, while she finds projects focused on corporate social media campaigns less engaging. This emotional intelligence guided her to specialize in green marketing, leading to both career growth and personal fulfillment.

Relationship and Social Decisions

Apply harmonization to interpersonal decisions.

• Which relationships energize or drain your emotional system?

• How do social commitments influence your emotional weather patterns?

- What boundaries should be established based on emotional wisdom?

- How can you express emotional needs without manipulation?

Financial and Lifestyle Decisions

Combine emotional intelligence with practical decisions.

- What does your emotional reaction to spending reveal about your values?

- How do various lifestyle choices impact your emotional health?

- What financial choices support or stress your emotional well-being?

- How can financial choices mirror genuine values instead of fear or status?

Financial Harmony Example: Marcus felt anxious about money when dining at expensive restaurants, but cooking for friends brought him joy and a way to connect. This emotional awareness led him to host dinner parties instead of eating out often, which bettered both his finances and social life.

Workplace Harmony in Complex Situations

Managing Team Conflicts

Situation: Two department heads disagree over the allocation of resources, which affects your project timeline.

Emotional Weather: Frustration from delays, anxiety over deadlines, concern about choosing sides.

Morning Coffee

Harmonized Response: "I I know both departments have important needs. I want to ensure we can deliver quality work on time. How about we focus on finding a solution that meets both your priorities and our project requirements?

This response recognizes the frustration caused by the delay issue; additionally, it reduces anxiety by emphasizing solutions, aiming to find a balance for project needs.

Navigating Organizational Change

Scenario: Your company announces a restructuring that may affect your role.

Emotional Weather: Feelings of fear about job security, anger over poor communication, excitement about potential new opportunities, and sadness regarding changes to current team dynamics.

Integration Strategy:

• Use fear as a motivator to develop skills and expand your network.

• Channel your anger into providing constructive feedback and improving communication.

• Go and explore new possibilities, keeping your commitment.

• Give yourself time to grieve and appreciate your current relationships before things change.

Handling Difficult Client Demands

Situation: The client requests substantial changes to the ongoing project at a late stage in its development.

Emotional Weather: Feelings of anger over moving goalposts, anxiety about the timeline's impact, frustration with scope creep, and a little excitement for creative challenges.

Harmonized Approach: "I appreciate your vision for these enhancements. Let me help you understand the implications for timeline and budget, and we can explore which changes offer the most value within our constraints."

This response recognizes the creative energy that comes from using anger and frustration as signals pointing out boundaries that need clarification.

The harmonization step transforms your emotional weather from being something that happens to you into information that guides conscious living. When you learn to understand emotional messages and use them as practical wisdom, every decision becomes an intuitive expression.

As you improve your skill in harmonization, you'll find that your emotions are not barriers to clear thinking but refined guidance systems that enrich every part of your life. The emotional weather that once felt overwhelming becomes a reliable partner in creating a life aligned with your deepest truth and highest wisdom.

CHAPTER 9: E - EMBODY NATURAL FREEDOM

True freedom isn't something you achieve. It's what happens when you stop getting in your own way. After months of practicing the WEATHER Method, you've likely noticed a real shift. Instead of using techniques every time you feel something, you simply notice emotions as they come and go, like clouds in the sky. You don't need to chase spiritual achievement—any understanding you've found was always there.

To embody freedom is to make emotional mastery as natural a process as breathing.

A common pitfall for those who have come far is turning emotional freedom into a new identity to uphold. You might catch yourself thinking, "I don't get triggered anymore," or feeling a bit proud of your emotional balance. Ironically, this sense of spiritual ego is what gets in the way of true freedom.

To truly embody freedom, let go of trying to prove your emotional mastery to anyone, even yourself. You stop checking your reactions to see if they're spiritually correct.

. . .

Some signs that show you are performing rather than embodying

- Monitoring your reactions in conversations, to be sure you're being "enlightened".
- Feeling disappointment when you respond emotionally and not consciously.
- Hiding struggles because they do not align with your spiritual identity.
- Using spiritual terms for mundane experiences.

The antidote is to be completely honest about your experience. When you stop pretending to be free emotionally, true freedom will come naturally.

Workplace Example: Sarah, a meditation teacher, lived through this during company layoffs. Instead of perpetually maintaining her calm exterior whilst internally panicking about job security, she let herself feel utter uncertainty and fear of professional instability. "I stopped being a spiritual teacher and started being a human employee," she shared. "That was the moment when I found the wisdom on how to navigate this situation skillfully."

Kind of Freedom Embodied

You drink your coffee and check your emotional weather as automatically as you check the external weather before choosing clothes.

There is no spiritual performance—just natural awareness.

If your boss gives you an unrealistic deadline, you might feel frustrated, but you respond with clarity instead of just reacting. You no longer feel the need to be the 'spiritual one' at work.

You may feel anxious about the expense while making practical choices for your actual circumstances, rather than reacting emotionally.

The Three Stages of Natural Integration

Stage 1: Conscious Application (Weeks 1-8)

You apply the WEATHER steps deliberately each time an emotion arises. You may have set phone reminders for emotional check-ins or started purposely pausing before responding to triggers.

Workplace Marker: You remember to include the 5-second pause during tricky meetings, even though it still feels like a conscious choice rather than an automatic action.

Stage 2: Fluid Response (Weeks 9-16)

The process becomes more natural. You find yourself witnessing emotions, exploring feelings, and just accepting the storm, so to speak, without any conscious effort. The steps blend into one natural process.

Professional Marker: In an intense project deadline, anxious feelings rise, and you begin to manage them while supporting others in the team without ever thinking consciously of any emotional tools.

Stage 3: Embodied Freedom (Weeks 17+)

The WEATHER method dissolves into your being. You are no longer employing techniques; instead, you are living in emotional freedom. Responses spring spontaneously from wisdom, with no conscious application of any framework.

Integration Marker: Colleagues suggest that you are more grounded and present, yet you are unable to pinpoint what you are doing differently.

For most people, progress feels more like an upward spiral than a straight path. Some days, you'll act naturally from Stage 3, while on others, you'll need to use the basics from Stage 1. This is normal and doesn't mean you're going backward.

Recognizing Your Integration Benchmarks

Daily Life Indicators:

• Emotional storms pass through you as weather would through an open sky.

• You feel intense emotions but cannot allow them to control you.

• Others say that you seem more present and grounded.

• You act out of clarity instead of emotional reactivity.

• Conflicts seem manageable instead of frightening.

Relationship Markers:

• You can hear criticism without pitching a defense.

• People feel comfortable sharing their genuine feelings around you.

• You stay centered through their emotional storms.

• Intimacy deepens because you are genuinely present, not just performing.

Professional Markers:

• You never take work stress home.

• You deal with difficult colleagues in your way without creating internal drama.

• Decision-making becomes clearer and more intuitive.

• Without effort, you radiate calm energy in stressful situations.

Advanced Workplace Integration

As you become more confident in your freedom at work, you naturally develop into what organizational psychologists call an 'emotional stabilizer.' Your presence alone enhances your team's ability to collaborate effectively.

During Crisis Management: Your innate emotional stability prevents the team from spiraling into collective panic when a client raises a major complaint. You are not trying to calm anyone down, but this centeredness creates space for clear thinking.

During Performance Reviews: Despite the challenging nature of the information, being present comes naturally whether you receive or give feedback; this presence makes difficult conversations more productive and less personal.

Managing Up: When your superior is stressed or demanding, you can feel their pressure but not take it on as an actual emergency. This enables you to be helpful to them without getting embroiled in their emotional weather.

Energy Management: You instinctively recognize which meetings, projects, and colleagues truly engage you and which ones drain your emotional resources. These insights guide your scheduling and commitments, avoiding strict rules or grand declarations.

Communication Boundaries: You can openly express your needs and concerns without falling into emotional manipulation or spiritual superiority. "I work best with some advance notice on urgent projects" is simply a factual statement, not a defense.

Collaborative Presence: In a team, you contribute ideas not to boost your ego, but genuinely from insight, aimed at serving the project's goals rather than seeking to appear wise or creative.

Even after adopting these practices, old habits may still surface, especially during stress, illness, or major life changes. The key is how you relate to these moments now.

Instead of spiritual self-judgment ("I thought I was past this"), you engage with a gentle curiosity: "Interesting, this old pattern is visiting! What might my system need right now?"

Emergency Integration Protocol

- Notice without judgment: "I'm having a very human moment."
- Return to basics: Use the five-second pause and basic witnessing.
- Seek appropriate support: Call a friend, take a walk, or rest.
- Extract the wisdom: What is this episode teaching you about current needs?
- Recommit gently: Return to natural practices without forcing.

Working example: Marcus, a corporate lawyer, found himself yelling at the computer during a very stressful time. Instead of spiraling into shame for failing spiritually, he took the afternoon off, went for a walk, and used the episode as a chance to reflect on unsustainable work habits. "The reactivity was a messenger telling me to reassess my boundaries," he realized.

Seamless Daily Integration

True embodiment means you no longer think of somebody's spiritual practice as something set apart from natural living. Every moment becomes an opportunity for presence.

Kitchen Consciousness

Washing dishes becomes present-moment awareness. Feel the warm water, notice if frustration arises about the mess, and witness whatever emotions arise without trying to change them.

Commute Meditation

Mindful awareness on the way to work: When you feel road rage coming on because someone cuts in front of you and you feel the irritation somewhere, you choose a response without turning it into a lesson of enlightenment.

Workbook Presence

Business-level conversations are genuinely connecting opportunities. You listen with all your being, speak honestly with all your being, and remain centered during confrontation, without adding spiritual posturing.

Bedtime Integration

Setting for sleep comes with natural emotional check-ins. Notice any worry or excitement from the day and allow the feeling to be; then, sleep without requiring perfect inner states.

Instead of worrying about whether your feelings match certain spiritual standards, you can accept whatever emotions arise. Trust your own understanding to guide you.

When your embodied freedom stabilizes into the center of your being, you become a potential source of calm for the anxious world. It is not because you are trying to help; rather, it is your very presence that makes a difference. People feel safe in your presence because you are not trying to fix them or promote your spirituality at their expense.

Your presence is the teaching; the others witness the person who can stay centered during difficulties without losing touch with humanity. This gives them hope and inspiration without the pressure for conversion.

Workplace Service Examples

During Team Conflicts: Your natural ability to remain non-reactive empowers others to express their perspectives without escalation. You are not mediating—you show by example what a calm presence sounds like in disagreement.

With Struggling Colleagues: When a team member encounters difficulties in their personal life, your sincere availability without expectation gives them time to process without feeling managed or judged.

In High-Pressure Situations: The emotional stability you embody during high-pressure deadlines or crisis management acts as an anchor with perspective, which keeps the team together effectively.

. . .

The real sign of embodied freedom is when you stop thinking about being spiritual. Days go by as you work, love, and play. You no longer try to be a spiritual person—you just live.

This doesn't mean losing wisdom or reverting to pre-conditioned reactive tendencies. This wisdom is so well integrated that applying it feels as natural as walking or talking.

Spiritual maturity, in its truest form, means having no spirituality. You respond spontaneously to life situations with natural wisdom, without spiritual posturing or performance. The other person may not know why, but somehow, they feel much more at ease in your company.

Maintaining Integration During Challenges

Sometimes, life throws challenges your way that test every part of your emotional freedom, like illness, breakups, job changes, or family crises. In these moments, your integration might look different, but it's still possible.

Crisis Integration Strategies:

• Temporarily lower standards: Get yourself in the presence of the crisis rather than reacting perfectly.

• Use the support systems passionately: Do not feel morally incapacitated to call on a friend, family, or professional.

• Go back to basics: Breathing exercises, walking, or resting; nothing more complicated.

• Trust the process: Big life storms sometimes take time to completely weather.

Emotional freedom now serves purposes beyond simply finding peace of mind. Through embodied presence, you help create space for others to discover their natural freedom. This often happens unintentionally and involuntarily just by you being genuinely yourself in everyday life. The search is over; living has begun, and it continues through extraordinary ordinariness—being present with whatever life presents before us.

CHAPTER 10: R - RADIATE AUTHENTIC PRESENCE

True emotional freedom shows when you stop trying to act spiritual and simply live it. This final step of the WEATHER method is where all your inner work naturally becomes a gift to those around you. Your emotional mastery is no longer just a personal goal. It becomes a real presence that shapes your relationships and community.

Having fully internalized the WEATHER framework, you will radiate as a source of solace in the emotional realm. It is not that you set out to instruct or remedy anyone; your sincere presence allows space for others to find their own freedom.

People who have found absolute emotional freedom often feel pressured to become spiritual teachers or guides for others. Friends and family can tell something is different about you now: Your cool-headed responses to interpersonal quarrels, workplace stress, or simple acceptance of the ups and downs. Everybody in town suddenly wants to know your secret.

A little pressure can accompany this newfound attention. The ego likes to claim ownership of any spiritual advancement, slipping into a teaching attitude that respects spiritual performance over genuine sharing. You find yourself giving away wisdom at dinner parties, suggesting different meditation methods to troubled colleagues, or feeling it is your responsibility to mend everybody's emotional messes.

The paradox is that the freer you become, the less you need to talk about it. Your actions and reactions show your freedom in daily life. Others notice a sense of relief and acceptance around you, and they feel more able to be themselves. This happens naturally, without your trying.

The paradox shows the difference between spiritual attainment and spiritual embodiment. Attainment involves the consciousness of "having" something that might be lost or maintained. Embodiment issues forth from the being. When emotional freedom is a state of being rather than an achieved state, you stop performing and start living it.

The Art of Humble Service

One of the challenges for emotionally free individuals is helping others without feeling spiritually superior.

Such humility is expressed in the following ways:

Sharing your struggles honestly: When asked about your calm presence, you can be honest about your humanity. "I still get triggered sometimes, but I've learned some approaches that help me work with difficult emotions differently." This normalizes the journey instead of mystifying it.

Avoiding spiritual diagnosis: Refrain from analyzing others' emotional patterns or telling them what they "need" to work on.

Instead, support them in feeling safe with whatever they are experiencing in the moment.

Leading by asking questions: Rather than providing solutions, ask thought-provoking questions that enable others to discover their own wisdom.

"When faced with stress like this, how would you typically handle it?" and "What feels most supportive to you right now?"

Admitting your limitations: Being honest about what you know and what you don't know, and recommending professional help for others. "That sounds like a difficult situation; maybe you could consider talking to someone who specializes in this?"

Emotional safety is the greatest gift you can give to others. When people feel safe around you, they can be themselves without worrying about being judged, manipulated, or overwhelmed by your emotions. You don't need special techniques for this; it comes from within.

Think of the difference between:

Unsafe Response: "Oh, you shouldn't feel that way! Have you tried meditation? I used to struggle with that too, but then I learned this technique..."

Safe: "That sounds really difficult. I can see how much this is affecting you."

This safe response is pure presence without any agenda. It refrains from minimizing the person's experience, offering premature solutions, or shifting attention to one's own journey.

Creating Safety Through Your Nervous System

. . .

Emotional safety operates at the level of the nervous system, even before conscious awareness is engaged. If your nervous system is truly calm and regulated, others' nervous systems will begin to co-regulate with you.

Creating Practical Emotional Safety

• Steady, calm breathing that stays even, no matter how others are feeling.

• A relaxed and open posture, even during difficult conversations.

• A steady voice that does not change, even if others are very emotional.

• Listening patiently, without hurrying to respond or offer advice.

• Facial expressions that stay non-reactive and present, rather than reflecting distress.

The most reliable way to create emotional safety is through "openness listening": giving full presence to another person without an agenda, advice, or the need to solve for them.

Authentic presence means:

• Focusing on the underlying feeling behind the words rather than just the words themselves.

• Maintaining focus on their experience without taking it on as your own.

• Letting silence surface after the other person is done speaking instead of rushing to fill it with one of your responses.

• Reflecting what you heard without any interpretation or advice: "It sounds like you're feeling overwhelmed by all these changes."

• Trusting the person to have the capacity to find their own solutions rather than presuming they need answers from you.

Morning Coffee

When a person is listened to in this way, they naturally access their clarity and wisdom.

Workplace Applications of Authentic Presence

Professional settings continuously present opportunities to radiate authentic presence without compromising your career development.

Team Leadership Through Presence

When a project is under pressure, your calmness helps others face challenges instead of joining in the group panic. You are not trying to manage anyone's emotions. Your steady presence simply creates space for clear thinking.

Example: In performance discussions, staying calm helps to create a space where you can accept feedback without getting defensive. This way, you can discuss challenging issues without resorting to personal attacks.

Managing conflicts: During disagreements between team members, your non-reactive presence enables all parties to express their views without escalating the situation. You are not mediating; instead, you model how a calm presence can be maintained in the face of disagreement.

Serving Colleagues Without Overextending

When someone shares personal struggles: "That sounds challenging to me. Thanks for sharing. What type of support is best right now? Something more along the lines of a sympathetic ear or brainstorming potential solutions?"

During workplace drama: "I can tell this situation is causing stress for everyone. I'll focus on my part of the project and trust that you all can work it out."

When a team member is overwhelmed: "I've noticed you might be dealing with a lot. Would it be helpful if I took over the task?

Professional Boundaries

Creating emotional safety does not mean you have no boundaries or that you are responsible for someone else's feelings. Healthy boundaries are essential for lasting support. They protect your energy and give others the freedom to be themselves.

Time boundaries: "I have about fifteen minutes to talk right now, but I want to really listen during that time."

Capacity boundaries: "I care about you, and I'm not in a space where I can hold something this intense right now. Can we connect about this tomorrow?"

Role boundaries: "This sounds like something that might benefit from professional support. I'm here as your colleague/friend, not as a therapist."

Energy boundaries: "I notice I'm starting to take on your worry as my own. Let me take a breath and come back to being present with you."

Maintaining Boundaries While Serving

Knowing whether you're truly helping someone or just enabling codependent habits is really important. Sometimes, the best help is actually just stepping back, especially if your help stops them from building their own emotional strength.

Offer Support When

- A person explicitly asks for your help.

- The person needs immediate crisis community support.

- Your support empowers the person to work out their own problem rather than having the support substituted.

- You can do so without consuming your own sources of strength.

Step back when

- Your help is another excuse for them to avoid proper professional help.

- You became more involved than they are.

- Helping others is breeding resentment and exhaustion inside you.

Signs of unhealthy dependence

- Someone asks for your help, but does not want to take action themselves.

- People get all upset whenever you are not there to help.

- Your emotional state will significantly affect their well-being.

- Others expect you to always be "the stable one" in every situation.

The Ripple Effect of Authentic Presence

Your levels of emotional freedom expand like ripples stretching out into the distant horizon. When you regularly express your true emotions, you encourage others to do the same.

Immediate Circle: Family and Close Friends

- Family members feel safe to express their honest feelings around you.

- Friends get more comfortable because they feel you will neither judge nor absorb their emotional experiences.

- Children react to emotional freedom because they can tell when adults are being genuinely present or just performing.

Professional Circle: Colleagues and Clients

- Colleagues may notice that you stay calm under pressure and begin to incorporate some of your strategies into their own behavior.

- Your presence brings comfort to the group; less anxious people work together more smoothly.

- Your authentic presence and clear boundaries enhance client relations.

Community Circle: Further Social Connections

- Your presence creates a fully healed emotional environment within social groups.

- Others begin to embrace the freedom to be genuine instead of adhering to social politeness.

- When making community decisions, wisdom prevails when emotions don't cloud judgment.

Unknown Circle: Strangers and Brief Encounters

Sometimes, brief moments of human connection occur during everyday interactions. Although fleeting, these moments can leave a lasting impression, even in busy environments like heavy traffic or crowded public spaces. Small, often spontaneous acts of kindness can inspire someone to reflect on human goodness, highlighting how simple gestures can have meaningful impacts.

People can influence others simply by being there, without necessarily taking specific actions or giving instructions. Often, others react to the emotions they perceive in someone, even if they can't quite articulate the subtle signals they pick up.

Maintaining Healthy Support

• Keep modeling how to be emotionally free and gently encourage others to acquire that skill.

• Provide others with resources, including this book, instead of always being their primary resource.

• Practice saying no to requests for support when help provided is not genuine.

• Encourage others to develop a broader network of support, rather than focusing all the support on you.

Daily Practices for Radiating Presence

An authentic presence is not something you turn on when entering a formal encounter; instead, it emerges through daily practices that keep you energetically connected to emotional freedom.

Early Morning Set Intention

Begin the day by setting an intention to stay calm and composed in any emergency, while maintaining emotional freedom. An intention might sound like: "Today I choose to offer my Authentic Presence while staying grounded in my own emotional freedom."

Presence Check-ins

Periodically check in with yourself throughout the day to see if you're genuinely present or just offering spiritual help. Ask yourself: "Am I trying to help from ego, or is it from genuine care? Am I keeping my emotional boundaries intact?"

Reflection into the Night

Think about times when you helped others just by being there for them. Consider also the moments when you might have taken on too much or focused more on how you appeared rather than being genuine.

Weekly Boundary Check-In

Once a week, assess your energy levels and the sustainability of your service to others. Are you giving from abundance, or are you depleting yourself? What could support a more sustainable way of serving?

Integration with the Ordinary Life

The best way to demonstrate genuine presence in everyday interactions is by being emotionally free. When you are truly yourself, you can support others more effectively.

With family: When your teenager opens up about their troubles, do not shut them down immediately or get emotionally activated by the intensity of their experience. Your presence allows them the space to process their own feelings.

In the community, attend local events with genuine interest and a sense of purpose, rather than out of duty; your calmness enhances collaboration and problem-solving.

This integration marks the end of your journey with the WEATHER Method. Emotional freedom is no longer something you have to practice; it has become so natural that it is a gift to everyone you meet.

As you move forward, remember that shining with genuine presence isn't another spiritual achievement to uphold; instead, it is the natural expression of who you have always been beneath the emotional storms that once seemed to define you. This emotional freedom now serves a greater purpose beyond personal peace—it helps heal a world that desperately needs examples of what becomes possible when human beings stop fighting themselves and begin working with the natural intelligence of their hearts.

CHAPTER 11: WORKPLACE AND FAMILY DYNAMICS

The relationships that challenge us most often teach us the most. The sense of emotional freedom you might feel during a quiet morning coffee is truly put to the test at work and with family. These close connections bring out your emotional habits and show you how your feelings interact with the moods of those around you.

This chapter investigates the top two environments where the spiritually advanced seeker typically finds it difficult to remain emotionally balanced: work, where you spend most of your waking hours, and family relationships, which crystallize your very first emotional patterns.

Your workplace isn't an enemy—it's your practice ground for emotional mastery. Most people see their professional environment as a spiritual obstacle course, with difficult colleagues, impossible deadlines, and killer politics that drain their very soul.

They feel as if they must choose between a state of inner peace and professional success, as though one has to exist in an entirely separate world from emotional freedom and career advancement. The false dichotomy has set many spiritually minded professionals up as double agents in life, hiding behind corporate facades while yearning for spaces where they truly feel alive.

But what if your workplace could actually become the most powerful environment for emotional growth you could ever imagine?

Advanced Workplace Emotional Dynamics

Managing up during organizational stress: Your boss becomes increasingly demanding, less available, and fairly unreasonable in his expectations as pressure from senior leadership rises. Your emotional wisdom becomes crucial to maintain professional effectiveness and your well-being.

Emotional intelligence strategy: Instead of taking their stress personally or getting defensive about their increased demands, let your emotional awareness guide your professional behavior.

• If you feel protective of your boundaries: "I want to support you during this busy period. Help me to understand your priorities so I can focus my energy most effectively."

• If you feel overwhelmed with the requests: "I want to focus on quality. With the current workload on us, what project do you think should be the priority?"

Helping Teams Handle Emotional Challenges

When teams face tight deadlines and uncertain situations, these emotional patterns demand your serious attention. Your emotional stability helps everyone feel secure, which benefits the team.

Team Weather Patterns:

- Deadline Panic: A collective anxiety that creates rushed decisions and poor communication.

- Change Resistance: Group opposition to new processes or leadership choices.

- Conflict Avoidance: Unresolved team tension affecting productivity and morale.

- Success Pressure: Perfectionism and interpersonal competition caused by high-stakes projects.

Leadership through emotional wisdom: "I can see this timeline is creating pressure on everyone. Let's take a moment to identify what is essential and support each other to deliver quality work while maintaining our sanity."

This response recognizes the shared emotional experience while offering practical advice to support both project success and team well-being.

Client and Customer Relationship Mastery

Difficult client management: When clients become demanding, unreasonable, or emotionally reactive, your emotional freedom becomes a valuable professional asset that supports their success.

Scenario: A major client calls an emergency meeting to voice dissatisfaction with the team's work, losing composure, and criticizing the team in a tone of frustration for not meeting expectations.

Professional Emotional Response:

- Witness: Notice your defensive reactions, as well as the urge to justify your team's efforts.

- Explore: What real concerns might be hidden beneath their emotional intensity?

- Accept: Their frustration is valid to them whether or not you accept their assessment as accurate.

- Harmonize: "I I understand you're concerned about the project direction, but please clarify specifically where your expectations weren't met so we can work on resolving those issues points."

This validates their emotional reality, yet it brings the conversation into a more concrete realm of problem-solving.

Sales and negotiation applications

Emotional freedom transforms sales interaction from manipulation into a genuine desire to provide service. Not being emotionally attached to specific outcomes enables you to:

- Pay attention to what is being said; listen to the client's needs instead of imposing predefined solutions them.

- Handle objections without taking them personally or becoming defensive.

- Offer options that will benefit the client and will increase your commission.

- Build a connection through authenticity instead of superficial enthusiasm.

Workplace Boundaries That Serve Everyone

Email and Communication Boundaries:

- Time-based boundaries: "I check emails at 9 am, 1 pm, and 4 pm to provide timely responses. If it is urgent, please call or text."

- Scope boundaries: "I want to make sure this meeting is productive. Could we please have an agenda and a time limit?"

- Energy boundaries: "I work best if I receive advanced notice of urgent projects. What systems can we build to help with that planning?"

Meeting and Collaboration Boundaries

• Focus boundaries: "I'd like to give this conversation the proper attention. Could we table the budget conversation until we've agreed on a timeline?"

• Emotional boundaries: "I feel a lot of frustration in this room. Let's take ten minutes to clear our heads."

• Decision-making boundaries: "I want to think about this proposal carefully and get back to you tomorrow to discuss next steps."

Family Weather Systems

Your family knows exactly where to press your buttons because they put them there. This is a truth that hits every spiritual seeker the moment they walk through their childhood front door, watching cultivated emotional freedom fade faster than morning mist. Within minutes of arriving at a family gathering, you might find yourself reacting with defensive patterns you thought you had moved beyond years ago.

Family relationships become the graduate school of emotional mastery, where theory is truly tested and turned into practical wisdom in the toughest arena.

Each family operates like a distinctive weather system of emotions, with patterns that occasionally recur and sometimes shift abruptly with the seasons. Similar to the weather outside, it exists beyond human control and demands anticipation and thoughtful responses.

Family Weather Patterns

- Pressure Systems: These unspoken tensions simmer for long periods, creating an atmosphere where everyone feels on edge, yet nobody directly discusses them.

- Emotional Storms: Emotions are bottled up for a long time only to eventually explode, often triggered by some petty incident—a hurricane releasing years' worth of unheard feelings.

- Seasonal Patterns: Emotional weather that tends to recur just before holidays, birthdays, or anniversaries, since people might want to pick a day or two to remember.

- Generational Climate: These are long-term emotional patterns inherited through family history that influence current interactions.

Family Role Weather Patterns

Understanding your specific family role helps clarify the emotional dynamics involved. Each role has its own typical triggers and patterns.

The Oldest Child Weather:

- Responsibility storms: You feel responsible for everyone else's happiness and family functioning.

- Performance pressure: Feeling the pressure to be a role model while managing your own struggles.

- Control Frustration: Anxiety that surfaces when family chaos breaks through despite your efforts to maintain control.

Family Integration Script: "I notice that I'm feeling responsible for fixing this situation. I can care about my family without taking on the burden of managing their every emotion."

The Middle Child Climate:

- Invisible weather: Feeling invisible or unheard in family conversations.

- Peacekeeping pressure: Constantly working to avoid conflict within the family.

- Comparison storms: Comparing yourself to siblings' achievements.

Integration response: "I matter in this family exactly as I am. I don't need to prevent conflict to have value."

The Youngest Child Playbook:

- Dismissed-weather: Not being listened to in family decisions.

- Depend-upon-me expectations: Family treating them as if they were incapable of anything for their age.

- Overreacting storms: The tantrums are to prove their independence and maturity.

Boundary Script: "My voice and perspective matter. I can assert myself without the melodrama."

Practical Family Conversation Navigation

If family members criticize your spiritual path: Instead of becoming defensive or explaining your practices, try saying, "I understand that you're concerned about me, and I appreciate that you care. This path brings me peace and helps me to become a better person."

If family members trigger old patterns: Rather than reverting to automatic childhood-based reactions, consider saying: "I'm noticing this conversation is triggering some intense feelings for me right now. Would you be okay with taking a short break and returning to it later?"

When family drama surfaces near you: Instead of getting drawn into the conflict, siding with either party, try saying, "I see how important this is for both of you; I will step away now and let you work it out together."

When family members share problems and ask for solutions, instead of offering quick advice or trying to fix everything, you could say: "That sounds challenging. Would it be more helpful to have someone just listen or to work on brainstorming some solutions?"

Holiday and Family Gathering Survival

Important events intensify the emotional climate within families. Here is how to get through these periods among storms:

Before the Event:

• Set realistic expectations for family interactions.

• Plan self-care strategies and exit routes.

• Practice key phrases for boundaries.

• Connect with your support system outside the family.

During the Event:

• Do weather check-ins for feelings regularly.

• Use bathroom or kitchen breaks for centering purposes.

• Practice pausing for five seconds before reacting.

• You can authentically engage without being forced to fake a happy face.

After the Event:

- Process what happened without any judgment.
- Identify factors that worked well and those that need to change.
- Have some self-compassion for the times when you reacted.
- Draw some lessons from the difficult interactions.

Setting Boundaries Without Creating Drama

The harmonization phase combines your spiritual insight with genuine love for family members, even when their actions conflict with their limiting beliefs. This process requires developing advanced emotional skills that honor both your authenticity and your family connections.

Energy Boundaries:

- Come into the family gathering well-rested and centered.
- Take breaks during the gathering to reconnect with your inner state.
- Limit time spent at emotionally draining visits.
- Create space without much explanation when necessary.

Communication Boundaries:

- Decide on which family conversations to engage fully and which to negotiate diplomatically.
- Redirect repeat complaints: "We've discussed this before. What would you like to be different now?"
- Limit advice giving: "I trust you to figure out what's best for your situation."

- Maintain topic boundaries: "I'd rather not talk about my personal relationships at family dinners."

Emotional Boundaries:

- Do not fix the emotional weather of a family member.

- Let family members experience their own consequences so that they can be accountable for their acts.

- Share your emotional weather, but don't expect the family to understand.

- Seek support outside the family system if needed.

Supporting Family Without Taking Responsibility

As you embody freedom, the family begins to open up more to you, sensing your acceptance without judgment. This creates opportunities to support their emotional growth without trying to fix or alter them.

When your teenage nephew opens up about social anxiety, listen without rushing to solutions. "That must be tough. What feels most supportive to you right now?" This helps him process while maintaining healthy boundaries.

When your elderly parent shares fears about aging: hold space for their vulnerability without cheerleading or offering empty reassurances. "I see how concerned you are about this. These feelings are justified."

When family members ask for advice: share your perspective and encourage them to trust their own wisdom. "Here's what I've experienced when faced with something similar; however, you know yourself better. What feels right to you?"

. . .

The Integration Challenge: Work-Family Balance

Spiritual intellectuals often struggle with compartmentalizing their lives. They feel that they need to be one person at work, another at home, and yet another during their spiritual practices. The WEATHER Method removes this tedious type of division by offering a single set of tools that work effectively in any situation.

Morning Integration: Begin each day by becoming aware of the emotional weather, which prepares you for both professional and personal interactions.

Transition Rituals: Create simple practices for shifting between work and family environments that respect and honor both.

Evening Integration: Conclude each day by processing emotional experiences from all contexts without separating "work emotions" from "family emotions."

Cross-Context Skill Transfer

Professional Skills Enhancing Family Life:

• Active listening techniques developed in client meetings improve communication with family.

• Setting boundaries in workplace negotiations supports healthy family dynamics.

• Conflict resolution in team management helps resolve family disputes.

Family Skills Enhancing Professional Performance:

• Practicing unconditional love in family relationships enhances connections with colleagues.

- Patience developed in dealing with family members strengthens client interactions.

- Nurturing authenticity within family circles strengthens leadership in the workplace.

When you start applying the WEATHER Method in your work and family lives, you'll begin to notice slow changes in some of your relationships—especially the unexpected ones. Family members who once triggered big reactions in you will gradually start to lose their grip on your emotional balance. Conversely, work-related conflicts that once seemed insurmountable may start to feel more genuine and connected.

The main goal isn't to fix your workplace or achieve perfect harmony with family. Instead, your top priority is to stay emotionally free while truly engaging in these relationships. You can have a positive impact on work and family dynamics while also supporting your own growth and well-being.

You can create spaces for unconditional love in your workplace and family. This means accepting your colleagues and family members as they are while still setting your boundaries and being true to yourself.

CHAPTER 12: WHEN STORMS RETURN

Storms don't care about your spiritual progress. This can be tough to accept, especially if you've been practicing the WEATHER Method and feeling good about your emotional growth, only to feel anger, anxiety, or grief again suddenly.

You might begin to question whether you've failed, if your progress was merely an illusion, or if the method isn't effective for you. These thoughts can become overwhelming, adding a second layer of difficulty—not due to the original emotion, but because of self-judgment and disappointment.

Just because you're going through a tough time emotionally doesn't mean you've failed. It simply means you're human—flawed, real, and beautifully genuine.

Many spiritual seekers hold onto a secret hope: that once they've really "done the work," they'll stay calm forever. But this idea can cause a lot of unnecessary suffering because it sets an impossible expectation. Even some of the most dedicated practitioners, those who've been meditating and exploring themselves for years, still find themselves struggling with difficult emotions. It's all part of the journey.

Sometimes, no matter how much we understand about the weather, it still changes unpredictably. The same goes for our emotions: they respond to things happening inside us and around us, influenced by seasons and sudden shifts. Instead of trying to make everything steady, it's healthier to accept these natural ups and downs, and focus on growing wiser and stronger through them.

Sarah, a dedicated meditation teacher, had been practicing WEATHER for three months when her company unexpectedly announced layoffs. Suddenly, she was overwhelmed by a wave of fear, anger, and uncertainty. Instead of using her skills to stay grounded, Sarah found herself inwardly chastising, thinking, "I should be handling this better. What kind of spiritual teacher gets this upset about job security?"

Sarah's poor reaction highlights a basic misunderstanding. She believed emotional mastery meant never experiencing strong feelings, instead of skillfully managing them when they occur. The corporate restructuring wasn't a sign of spiritual failure; it was an invitation to practice the WEATHER Method in conditions that would build her emotional resilience over time.

When old emotional patterns come back, it might feel like you're going backward. In reality, think of it as "integration testing." Life gives you opportunities to practice emotional freedom, even during tough times. Think of it like this—if you've been learning to drive in a parking lot, eventually you'll need to face real traffic to become street-smart. Emotional setbacks are similar; they are opportunities to see whether your practice holds up under real-world stress.

Common Situations That Trigger Emotional Storms

. . .

Life transitions that exceed the limits of adaptation: career change, shifts in relationships, health challenges, and family dynamics, all of which overwhelm your current ability to process. These situations put your emotional resilience to the test in ways that a calm practice period cannot.

Accumulated stress can really take a toll on us, sometimes reaching a breaking point. Over weeks or months, small stressors —like looming work deadlines, family responsibilities, and health worries—pile up, creating a perfect storm that overwhelms our emotional well-being.

Anniversary reactions and seasonal patterns are our unconscious responses to important dates, seasons, and life cycles. Our minds tend to remember losses, traumatic events, and big life changes, often creating emotional storms around these moments without us even realizing it.

Growth spurts in our awareness can sometimes feel overwhelming, impacting our emotions. It's perfectly okay to take breaks and give ourselves time to adjust. Plus, gaining new spiritual insights might temporarily shake our sense of stability as we work to understand these fresh ideas.

"When you recognize these patterns, you can observe setbacks with curiosity instead of judgment. Instead of thinking, "What's wrong with me?', you might wonder, "What lessons is this storm trying to teach me?'."

The WEATHER Method While Experiencing a Crisis

When those intense feelings resurface, you can still use the WEATHER Path as a guide, but it might need some adjustments to work well in such a high-stress moment. Remember, in emotional emergencies, the goal isn't to be perfect with your techniques—it's about doing whatever helps you stay grounded and keep your balance.

W—Emergency Witnessing

During emotional storms, it can feel overwhelming to just observe what's happening. Instead, go for micro-witnessing: take small moments to pause and reconnect with your awareness.

Take a moment to breathe deeply three times, softly letting go of any feelings with each exhale.

Body anchor technique: Feel your feet firmly on the ground or gently resting against a chair; a little bit of physical sensation can help anchor your awareness.

Name without blame: Name the emotion without applying commentary.

Emergency witnessing phrases:

- "I notice intense emotion moving through me."
- "This is a storm, not my permanent state."
- "I can feel this without becoming it."

E—Crisis Exploration

Exploration during deeply emotional moments calls for a gentle, almost nurturing attention. It's about focusing on the questions that truly matter.

- How does this emotional weather system come to be?
- Take note. Is there a deeper message in this emotion that I should pay attention to?

During a storm, it's probably not the best time to dive into deep thinking. It's better to save those reflections for when things settle down a bit. For now, just focus on gathering the basics—there's no need to understand everything right away.

A—Emergency Acceptance

Acceptance during an emotional storm is about gently letting go of the urge to fight what you're going through. It doesn't mean you enjoy or wish to stay in those feelings; rather, it's about stopping the struggle against what's happening and allowing yourself to simply be with it. Think of it as permitting yourself to be imperfect and to feel whatever comes up, without judgment or resistance.

Acceptance phrases during crisis moments:

- "This [emotion] is welcome here for as long as it needs to stay."

- "I don't have to like this feeling, but I can stop fighting it."

- "This storm is temporary weather in my permanent sky."

- "I'm strong enough to feel this completely."

When acceptance feels really tough, try gently reminding yourself that it's okay not to feel okay right now. Maybe you can softly tell yourself, "I'm having a hard time accepting this pain right now, and that's okay." Remember, sometimes giving ourselves permission to resist is a kind and caring act.

T—Crisis Transition Support

The transition stage can sometimes last longer than expected during especially intense emotional moments. Your role isn't to hurry the process but to foster the best environment for a natural flow.

Support for immediate transition:

- Make sure that basic human needs are met (food, water, rest, safety).

- Create physical comfort (blankets, comfortable clothes, calming atmosphere).

- Try to encourage gentle movements like walking, stretching, or swaying, in a way that feels easy and natural.

- Help your nervous system to feel more balanced and relaxed, using rhythms like drumming, music, or steady breathing to make it feel more natural and calming.

Remember, sometimes storms need to run their full course before things start to clear. Fighting against the natural timing often only makes the darkness last longer. Be gentle and patient with yourself during tough times.

H—Emergency Response Strategies

During storms, staying calm and taking care of yourself might be more important than making complex decisions.

Crisis response priorities:

- Focus on creating a safe and nurturing environment for yourself, where your needs—whether emotional or physical—are recognized and cared for. Prioritize safety and comfort as essential steps to well-being.

- To better support and connect with others, try incorporating calming practices like deep breathing, gentle movement, or grounding exercises to help manage overwhelming feelings.

- Social support - it's often just the right moment to reach out to friends, family, or professionals who can lend a helping hand.

- Consider taking a step back from some of our commitments for now. This way, we can free up time and energy to focus on what genuinely matters most to us.

- Take a moment after the storm passes to reflect on what it might be teaching you. Embrace these lessons and let them help you grow.

E—Crisis Embodiment

Being present during tough weather means acknowledging the experience without letting it overwhelm you. It's about staying connected to what you're feeling without getting lost inside it.

• Continue with basic daily activities while acknowledging the emotional weather.

• Allow the feeling to melt in without forcing positivity or spiritual performance.

• Maintain a gentle connection with your body through mindful movement.

• Practice self-compassion instead of self-improvement.

R—Authentic Crisis Sharing

During the emotional storm, instead of forced positivity, radiate complete authenticity:

• Honestly communicate to others what you can and cannot handle.

• Feel free to ask for the support you need, whenever you need it.

• Share your experience with no preaching or teaching.

The Emotional Storm Survival Kit

Just like how people gather emergency kits to handle natural disasters, putting together a personal emotional storm survival kit can help you stay calmer and more grounded when emotions run high.

Physicality Comfort Resources

Sensory Comfort Items:

• A soft or weighted blanket to help calm the nervous system.

- Clothes that feel comfortable and nurturing.

- Vintage scents: essential oils such as lavender, eucalyptus, or vanilla.

- Herbal teas or any beverages that can calm your system.

- Textures that ground you: smooth stones, soft fabrics, stress balls.

Nourishment Supports:

- Comfort food: easy-to-make dishes that are truly nourishing.

- Hydration reminders with quality water.

- Protein snacks to help stabilize your blood sugar.

- Emergency meal delivery services should be accessible during severe storms.

Emotional Support Resources

Human Connection:

- List of three to five trusted friends or family contacts.

- Talking with a therapist, counselor, spiritual director, or doctor can really help. These professionals support you through your journey to relief.

- Crisis helpline numbers should you face any emergencies.

- Interest-based online support communities or forums that feel safe to you.

Self-Support Tools:

- Voice recording of yourself sharing compassionate words with yourself.

- Photos or souvenirs that remind you of strength and love.

- Inspirational books, podcasts, or music to help restore perspective.

- Written notes about your values, accomplishments, and reasons for hope.

Practical Navigation Tools

WEATHER Reminders:

- Quick-reference cards with WEATHER framework.

- Pre-written compassionate statements for different emotions.

- Index cards of simple breathing exercises.

- An emergency checklist of self-care (shower, eat, sleep, walk, connect).

Perspective Restoration:

- Entries in your journal from storms you've weathered before.

- Letters from people who love or appreciate you.

- Proof of your growth and resilience over time.

- Mantras or phrases that ground you in truth.

Understanding Different Types of Emotional Weather Systems

Not all emotional weather systems are the same. Being able to discern the type of storm you are going through will help you set realistic expectations for recovery and apply the appropriate response to it.

Flash Floods (Sudden Unbearable Emotions)

When emotions hit, they can come on so suddenly and strongly that it feels like there's no escaping them—like they're triggered by something just barely noticeable. For example, sudden rage in a quarrel, panic attacks, acute grief reactions, violent jealousy, or fear.

Weather Response: Focus on staying calm and grounded right now—try breathing exercises and grounding techniques to help you feel safe. Remember, it's best not to overthink during a flood or emergency; there will be time to analyze and process everything afterwards.

Recovery Timeline: During the 20 minutes to 2 hours of peak intensity, residual phenomena may extend well beyond 24-48 hours.

Seasonal Storms (Predictable Emotional Patterns)

Characteristics: Emotional weather systems that return cyclically, usually in connection with anniversaries, seasons, or life transitions.

Examples: Anniversary-related grief, seasonal affective disorder, birthday-related anxiety, holiday-related stress patterns.

WEATHER Response: Whenever you can, try to get a head start. Think of your feelings like weather reports—use them to foresee upcoming storms, plan around them, and get ready for what's ahead.

Recovery Timeline: Variable, but mostly inclined to follow a path that you can trace over time.

Pressure Systems (Building Emotional Weather)

Characteristics: Over days or even weeks, you might notice your feelings gradually intensifying—often because of mounting stress or unresolved negative emotions. It's a common experience that many people go through.

Examples: Stress at work, tension in a relationship, or worries about money—these things can build up slowly over time, making each day feel a little heavier.

Weather Response: Early intervention really works. Pay attention to those tiny signals that might show stress building up — catching it early can prevent big problems later.

Recovery Timeline: Recovery really depends on how quickly you get help. If you start treatment early, usually it takes about 3 to 7 days to see improvements.

Perfect Storms (Multiple Stressors Converging)

Characteristics: Several big moments come together, making the emotions feel even more intense.

Examples: Losing your job while a family member is in crisis, juggling relationship issues alongside money worries, or dealing with health problems that seem even harder to face during big life changes — these are struggles that many people understand all too well.

WEATHER Response: Focus on tackling one challenge at a time instead of trying to handle everything all at once. It's okay to ask for help and to adjust your goals as needed.

Recovery Timeline: The duration can range from just a few days to several weeks, depending on how complex the situation is and how much support is available.

Self-Compassion As a Key in Emotional Storms

. . .

Morning Coffee

The way to navigate emotional storms is to be kind to yourself. Think of how you'd comfort a close friend who's going through a tough time — offer yourself that same warmth and understanding.

The Inner-Critic Storm

During difficult emotional times, you might hear that little voice inside your head analyzing what you might have done wrong.

- "You should be over this by now."
- "Other people handle this better."
- "You're supposed to be evolved."
- "This proves you haven't really learned anything."

Imagine your inner critic as someone shouting at you in the middle of a storm. They're trying to protect you, warning you about what's wrong. But honestly, all their shouting just makes you feel worse and makes it harder to find peace. In the middle of the chaos, they're not really your friend.

Replace harsh self-judgment with compassionate acceptance:

Instead of saying, "I'm pathetic for feeling this overwhelmed," try rephrasing it to sound more relatable and compassionate. You could say: "This is a tough moment, and it's completely normal to feel overwhelmed when you're facing [specific situation]. I'm doing my best with the resources I have right now."

Instead of saying, "I should be stronger than this," try expressing, "My strength lies in my ability to be vulnerable. My feelings show how much I genuinely care about what matters to me." This approach makes you more relatable by highlighting genuine emotions and human experiences.

Instead of saying, "I'm failing at spiritual practice," try rephrasing it as: "Learning to be with difficult emotions is part of my spiritual journey. This challenging time helps me develop genuine wisdom, not just theoretical knowledge." This approach makes the message more relatable and humanized.

When Professional Support Is Needed

While the WEATHER Method offers some really helpful tools to help you find emotional freedom, it's also okay to admit when you need a bit more support. Asking a professional for help during difficult times isn't a sign of weakness — it's a smart and caring choice for yourself.

Consider seeking professional support if:

- Emotional storms tend to last for more than one week without any relief.

- You're having thoughts of harming yourself or others.

- Use of substances increases during emotionally rough times.

- Your capacity to function at work or in relationships has been remarkably diminished for extended periods.

- You notice patterns of emotional abuse directed at yourself or others.

- Emotional storms are accompanied by physical symptoms (chronic insomnia, changes in appetite, physical pain).

- You have felt consistently hopeless about your capacity to change your relationship with emotions.

Types of Professional Support

. . .

Therapeutic Support:

• Trained and licensed therapists with skills in emotional regulation techniques.

• Trauma specialists if past experiences are affecting current emotional states.

• Group therapy oriented to emotional intelligence and emotional regulation.

Medical Support:

• Primary care doctors for physical symptoms accompanying the emotional storms.

• Psychiatrists, for a possible evaluation of medication in case support of brain chemistry is needed.

• Practitioners of integrative medicine, offering a more holistic approach.

Spiritual Support:

• Spiritual directors or counselors versed not only in emotional work but also in spiritual development.

• Meditation teachers trained in methods of working with challenging emotions.

• Religious or spiritual communities, which similarly offer down-to-earth emotional assistance.

Building Anti-Fragile Emotional Resilience

Most of us just want the emotional chaos to settle down so life can feel normal again. But there's actually more to it. Going through these tough times helps you build what researchers call 'antifragility' — in other words, becoming stronger because of the hard experiences.

Anti-fragile emotional resilience refers to:

• The more storms you have been through, the more confident you become in your ability to weather storms in the future.

• Difficult emotions become a source of wisdom and strength instead of merely problems to tolerate.

• Through your experience of emotional freedom, your ability to stand behind others increases.

• You develop unshakable trust in your ability to deal with anything life throws at you.

Marcus, the project manager, has been through a lot. Using the WEATHER Method to handle workplace crises, he's gained real experience and resilience. Now, during stressful moments, teammates look to him for guidance, knowing he's been through it all and can help everyone stay steady.

Long-Term View of Emotional Storms

As you become more emotionally free, you'll notice that how you deal with setbacks begins to shift. What once seemed like huge failures will soon feel more like just weather passing through—simply information about where you are right now.

The Spiral Flow of Emotional Growth

Emotional growth isn't a straight line. Think of it like climbing a spiral staircase—you might come back to some of the same feelings or issues, but each time from a slightly higher perspective.

When a familiar emotion pops up, it might feel like you're taking a step back. In reality, you're working through the same feelings but with better understanding and tools. Every time you encounter difficult emotions, you're actually moving closer to healing and greater self-awareness.

Cultivation of Weather Wisdom

Eventually, you will develop an intuition, "weather wisdom," that describes your emotional weather, so to speak, and guides you through it.

• Seasonal awareness - Knowing one's emotional rhythms and prepping for times of challenge when they are likely to arise.

• Storm prediction - Feeling the buildup of difficult emotional weather and working actively against it.

• Recovery knowledge - Understanding what draws one back into balance after the storm.

• Pattern recognition - Being able to identify deeper patterns and learnings in recurring emotional challenges.

CONCLUSION: YOUR NATURAL FREEDOM

The freedom you've always wanted has been right there each morning in your cup of coffee. This simple truth sums up your journey through these pages. You now see that the peace you were searching for through spiritual pursuits, books, and teachers wasn't hidden in a distant retreat or some future enlightened state. It was always here, in the ordinary moments you may have overlooked, like simply noticing your inner weather without trying to change it.

You've graduated from seeking to being.

Think back to who you were when you first picked up this book. Maybe you were a little worn out from chasing peace—always learning, always practicing, but never quite feeling like you could hold onto it. You'd read the books, gone to the workshops, listened to all the wise teachers. Yet, your emotions still ran wild sometimes, and the gap between what you knew and what you could actually live felt huge.

That version of you was caught in what I call the Spiritual Knowledge Trap—the idea that the next technique, the next insight, or just the right teacher would finally bring the freedom you wanted.

You probably thought awakening meant something dramatic, or needed perfect conditions, or years and years of effort to reach some future version of yourself.

The truth is far more straightforward and way more radical than you thought.

Through WEATHER, you've learned that emotional freedom isn't something you achieve—it's something you uncover. It was never about adding another practice to your routine or chasing more spiritual experiences. It's about learning to move with your feelings the same way you accept whatever weather rolls in.

Think about rain. You don't try to stop it or fix it—you just let it be. You don't blame yourself because you can't control the weather. You just notice whatever kind of rain it is, let it run its course, and then do what you need to do—grab an umbrella, stay inside, whatever works. You don't make it personal. The rain doesn't mean anything about you.

This natural wisdom now equally supports your inner weather. You have learned to be with emotions rather than being controlled by them.

The biggest change isn't in your circumstances—it's in how you relate to them. You're not an unsuspecting victim of your emotions anymore; you're an active part of your own inner weather system.

Before, when anxiety showed up, your mind would race—How do I get rid of this? What technique do I use? What am I doing wrong? Now you just notice—Oh, looks like it's anxiety weather. What might this be trying to tell me?

You are no longer the seeker forever trying so desperately to become something else. You are not the spiritual student forever striving to become better. Nor are you the damaged individual that must be fixed.

QUINN PATH

You're the awareness that's always there—no matter what the weather's doing.

You don't have to create awareness through any method—it's already part of who you are. The WEATHER Method just helped you notice what was always there. Each step brought you back to this natural ability—to witness, to explore, to accept, to change, to blend, to embody, and finally, to radiate presence.

You haven't turned into someone new—you've just stopped pretending to be someone you're not.

So what does life look like now that emotional freedom feels natural, not like an uphill battle? You can see it in all kinds of ordinary moments.

Your morning coffee isn't just about caffeine—it's a chance to be present. You might pause for a moment and notice how you feel, no agenda required.

Work stress doesn't hit you the same way. When something goes wrong, you know it's the pause—the space before you react—that makes all the difference. Responding with a little thought instead of lashing out leads to better outcomes every time. That's wisdom, not just habit.

Your relationships shift, too. You don't need other people to change for you to feel okay—and you no longer get swept up in their emotional weather.

Even money decisions come from a clearer place inside—not just panic or old habits. Your spiritual values and your practical side work together now.

Most importantly, you've stopped living a split life—spiritual when things are calm, reactive when life gets messy. The same awareness you bring to meditation is there when you're in a tough conversation at work or home.

Morning Coffee

With the method and the knowledge of your natural faculties for emotional freedom at hand, you now have three straightforward, clear choices:

1. Start today—with your next cup of coffee

No need to wait for perfect conditions. Your next coffee break—in five minutes or tomorrow morning—can be a chance to practice. Just:

- Take three conscious breaths before the first sip.

- Notice whatever "emotional weather" is there—no need to change it.

- Try saying, "This [emotion] is welcome here."

- Trust that even an ordinary moment like this has everything you need for real change.

2. Pick one WEATHER step to focus on this week

Don't try to do all seven steps perfectly. Just choose the one that feels most important for you right now.

If you feel reactive, use W (Witness) with a 5-second pause. If you get carried away in emotional stories, use the E (Explore) gently with curiosity. If you struggle with intense emotions, use the A (Accept) with welcoming phrases. If you enforce resolution: Use T (Transition) and trust its natural pace. If you are reacting instead of responding, use H (Harmonize) with wise choices in your spirituality. If you are being true to yourself, use E (Embody) with genuine authenticity. If you are sitting in isolation during hard times, use R (Radiate) through genuine presence with others.

3. Share your natural freedom

Your natural emotional freedom isn't meant to be a private thing —it's meant to be shared with the people around you. That doesn't mean you have to teach or preach. This is how you can share:

• Let a few close friends know you're trying something different with your emotions.

• Be real with your family about how you feel.

• Bring a little more presence to work conversations.

• Listen to people—really listen—with no agenda to fix them.

• Trust that when you're grounded, it helps others find their own footing, too.

Stop your search here; growth continues beyond this point. To sustain this progress:

For the First Month:

• Call upon the Quick Reference Guide (Appendix B) whenever emotions are challenging you.

• Go through the Daily Practice Integration Checklist (Appendix C) to build lifelong habits.

• Observe your emotional patterns by using the Weather Tracker (Appendix D) without judgment.

In Perpetuity:

• Associate with people who support emotional authenticity and conscious living.

• Continue to learn about emotional intelligence and healthy relationships.

• Find appropriate professional support with overwhelming challenges.

• Mastery means going deeper in your understanding. You cannot just be given it; you have to earn it.

When Storms Return (And They Will):

- Remember, these are natural weather variations, not spiritual failures.

- Return to the WEATHER Method with self-compassion, rather than with self-judgment.

- Use the info from your setbacks to evaluate your present needs, not your inadequacies.

- Believe that you naturally stand the test of any emotional climate.

Your emotions are now settled, and you've started to notice something pretty incredible. Somehow, just by being yourself, you influence the emotional mood of the people around you. You're not trying to teach, fix, or improve anyone—you're simply the steady center that helps calm their chaotic world.

This service is all about simply being there, rather than trying to do or fix. You're not pushing anyone to heal or pointing out what's wrong. Instead, it's about being fully present—emotionally free and naturally responsive to what each moment calls for.

Your emotional freedom initiates a series of concentric circles that release their influence on people's lives:

- Your immediate family will become a little more patient and understanding with each other, allowing for more genuine and heartfelt interactions.

- Your close friends will again feel safer to share their feelings.

- Your colleagues will see a new, more open way to work together, instead of feeling defensive.

- The community will be a bit more united, standing together in peace and order rather than falling into chaos and disorganization.

QUINN PATH

• And several strangers will gain a little unplanned yet genuine human contact.

You don't need to tell anyone about your transformation or convince others to follow your way. The world out there, longing for emotional clarity, often doesn't get to see your true, authentic self.

What a person might realize through this kind of work could be called "everyday enlightenment." It's when someone awakens to truly live life, embracing it fully instead of trying to escape from it. This isn't some dramatic flash of enlightenment that movies often depict. Instead, it's a gentle confidence—trusting that you can understand and handle whatever arises within your inner world. Your own enlightenment feels like:

• Drinking morning coffee with genuine presence.

• Responding to criticism without losing your center.

• Experiencing difficult emotions without being controlled by them.

• Choosing out of wisdom rather than fear.

• Remaining open-hearted while others close up.

• Being comfortable in ordinary moments instead of chasing extraordinary ones.

That is real enlightenment. You don't have to retreat to a cave, give up your everyday life, or aim for some impossible standard of spiritual perfection. Instead, it's about being fully present with whatever's happening right now. You can choose to connect with the natural wisdom inside you—your emotional guidance system—to help you navigate life's ups and downs.

What initially drew you to this book—the hope of transforming emotional overwhelm into spiritual freedom—has already been fulfilled. You've learned simple practices you can bring into your daily life, rather than just thinking about change. More importantly, you realize that this freedom—the sense of peace and clarity—is actually part of who you are, always been a part of you.

The search for something new to gain is over. In fact, it ends when you remember something that was never lost: your presence, your wisdom, your peace. These aren't dependent on outside conditions, spiritual achievements, or external environments—they're always within you, ready to be accessed whenever you need them.

You are the sky; the weather goes across it.

Every sip of coffee, every tough conversation, and every moment of joy or pain serve as gentle reminders to be present. Life's simple moments are actually powerful spiritual practices that guide us back to this truth. Conversely, these everyday experiences highlight the value of our spiritual journey.

The freedom you've been searching for isn't some distant, enlightened state; it's already within your reach, hidden in the simple act of being fully present with whatever arises. That morning coffee you savor today has as much potential for awakening as any retreat or meditation.

Even a difficult conversation holds the possibility for growth and wisdom, just like a spiritual teaching. It's all about seeing the divine in the ordinary, about recognizing that the path to awakening is right here, in the everyday moments we often overlook.

The weather keeps changing, whether or not you understand the science behind it. In the same way, your emotions follow their natural rhythms and cycles. The only difference now is that you see these emotional patterns not as personal crises, but as fascinating natural phenomena — part of the ebb and flow of life.

You've come to see a simple truth: real awakening happens in everyday moments, not just during special or extraordinary events. Each day offers countless small opportunities to cultivate presence, wisdom, and genuine expression. We don't need to call these acts 'spiritual practices'; they are just natural ways of responding to life as it happens.

Your journey isn't about reaching some far-off goal anymore. Instead, it's about coming home to yourself—who you've always been deep down, beneath the ups and downs of life's weather. The truly special parts of you are hidden in the everyday moments, just waiting to be recognized through a quiet, natural awareness that you've never truly lost.

The life you've experienced has led you here, not because you're on some spiritual quest, but because there's a simple miracle in just being fully present—whether it's a sunny day or a storm passing across the vast sky of your true self. The freedom you've always been searching for is right here, always has been. Welcome to your natural freedom.

AFTER THE LAST CUP

If you've reached this point, then you've spent some time noticing ordinary moments more carefully.

This book wasn't written to give you new beliefs to adopt or ideas to admire from a distance. It was written to help close the gap between knowing and being—to make emotional awareness something you can actually live, in the middle of ordinary days.

Readers take different things from this practice.

Some feel quieter.

Some more capable with difficult emotions.

Some simply more at ease with what shows up.

If *Morning Coffee* was useful to you—if the WEATHER Method helped you relate to your emotions with more clarity or kindness—I would appreciate you sharing a brief, honest Amazon review. Not a summary, just your experience of what changed, what helped, or what stayed with you.

Your reflection helps other readers know whether this approach might support them as well.

QUINN PATH

Thank you for reading.

And for meeting your emotional weather as it is, one ordinary moment at a time.

APPENDIX A

Your practical toolkit helps you turn understanding into everyday mastery over your emotions. These thoughtfully crafted resources connect what you learn about the WEATHER Method with actually applying it in real life. Many spiritual seekers find themselves stuck in a frustrating cycle of brilliant insights that seem to disappear the moment a real emotional storm hits. These Appendices are here to make sure that doesn't happen to you - they're designed to support you through both peaceful moments and emotional tempests.

Each tool is designed to help you navigate everyday moments, guiding you toward a sense of freedom from emotional and spiritual overwhelm. It's about supporting you in feeling more grounded and at peace in your daily life.

Appendix A

Fast Track Quick Start Guide

If you want to begin practicing right away and never get into this book:

The 5 Minutes Foundation

If you can set aside just five minutes each day to practice emotional freedom, start here.:

1. Choose Your Daily Anchor (1 min) Choose an activity you perform without fail every day:

- Having morning coffee or tea.

- Brushing your teeth.

- Checking the phone first thing in the morning.

- Walking to your car.

2. Build the Foundation Practice (3 mins) Carry out this simple sequence during your chosen activity:

- Take one conscious breath before beginning.

- Notice how you feel emotionally right now.

- Say silently: "This [emotion] is welcome here."

- Continue your activity with this awareness of emotional weather.

3. Put Your Intention Into Action (1 min) Commit yourself to doing this minimum practice for seven days and mark your calendar. This way, after one week, you can extend it if you want, but start ridiculously small.

The Essential WEATHER Framework

W - Witness: An observer, recognizing that once emotions arise, they need a witnessing pause of five seconds, without a reaction.

E - Explore: What might this emotion be trying to communicate to me? Instead of asking: How do I get rid of this?

A - Accept: It's good to say, "This [emotion] is welcome here" without trying to remedy it or change it.

T - Transition: Let emotions move on of their own accord; don't force them to resolve in a hurry.

H - Harmonize: Harmonizing with the emotional data to guide your behavior and decisions.

E - Embody: To operate from a place of emotional freedom as a natural state, sans spiritual showmanship.

R - Radiate: Sharing one's authentic presence with others, not preaching, nor teaching.

If overwhelmed by intense emotions:

1. STOP whatever you are doing

2. Take three conscious breaths

3. SIMPLY NAME the emotion: anger, fear, sadness

4. REMEMBER, this is weather, not your eternal identity

5. DECIDE your next step using any WEATHER tool that feels within reach

First Week Practice Schedule

Day 1-2: Focus on W only (Witnessing). Practice the 5-second pause with minor irritations.

Day 3-4: Add E (Explore). When feelings are stirred up, ask, "What is this telling me?"

Day 5-6: Add A (Accept). Practice saying, "This [emotion] is welcome here."

Day 7: During one emotional incident, practice the entire W-E-A sequence.

Signs That Let You Expand

Expanding will be possible after your first week if you notice:

- The 5-second pause happens of its own accord
- A genuine curiosity about emotions versus instant resistance
- Reduced urgency to heal or change the seemingly difficult feeling immediately
- Moments of spontaneous acceptance of emotions

Quick Troubleshooting

"I keep forgetting to practice" → Set phone reminders for your chosen daily anchor activity.

"It's not working." → Success is not eliminating emotions; it is altering your relationship to them.

"I don't have time" → Use existing activities and do not add new time commitments.

"My emotions are too intense." → First, start with smaller emotions; get professional help if needed.

Once you've gotten the hang of the Quick Start approach, try going back to Chapter 4 and take a closer look at the Witness step. After that, work your way through the entire method step by step. Keep in mind: real change comes from lots of small actions, not just a few big breakthroughs. That simple cup of coffee you enjoy every morning might have more potential to transform you than any fancy spiritual practice.

APPENDIX B

Quick Reference WEATHER Method Guide

Sometimes, when emotions surge and strike you like an unexpected thunderstorm, you need to have this handy framework ready and accessible without looking through detailed instructions. This set of notes aims to condense the entire WEATHER Method into a few simple, memorable core elements so you can find clarity even in darkness.

The 5-Second Emergency Response

Use this first step when the complete WEATHER method becomes too overwhelming:

1. STOP anything you are doing.

2. TAKE ONE CONSCIOUS BREATH.

3. TELL yourself what you feel: "anger," "fear," "sadness."

4. REMEMBER the feeling is the weather-it does not define you.

5. DECIDE on your next step out of the weather framework below.

QUINN PATH

W - WITNESS THE STORM

Core Action: To be aware without reacting immediately; say yes to the following Quick Steps:

- Use the 5-second pause before action

- Scan for emotional sensations

- Ask: "What am I feeling right now?"

That is to say, begin at the very top of your head and mentally sweep down, through the face and neck, into the shoulders, chest, arms, stomach, hips, legs, and down to the feet. Any tension, warmth, coolness, or other sensation?

E - EXPLORE THE LANDSCAPE

Core Action: Shift the person's mindset from "How do I fix this?" to What is this?"

Quick Steps:

- Look into what triggered that feeling or the deeper motivation for the feeling

- Observe your innate attitudes or actions towards it

- Ask: "What triggered this feeling?" and "What does this emotion want me to know?"

Curiosity Starters: "I notice that I am feeling..." "This reminds me of..." "My body is signaling me..." "The story I am creating is..."

A - ACCEPT THE WEATHER

Core Action: Welcome the emotion as a natural visitor

Quick Steps:

- Releasing the compulsion to change your state immediately

- Being reminded that emotions come and go and are not eternal

- Voicing out: "This [emotion] is welcome here" or "I accept what I'm feeling right now"

Acceptance Phrases:

- "This anger belongs here."
- "I make space for this sadness."
- "This anxiety is part of my current weather."
- "I don't need to fix this feeling."

T - TRANSITION WITH FLOW

Core Action: Allow natural emotional movements without forcing them

Quick Steps:

- Give it time
- Trust the timing of feelings
- Ask: "What does this emotion need to move naturally?"

Flow Reminders: Emotions have their own timing. Like weather systems, they move when conditions are right. Your job is not to control their movement but to grant them space to flow naturally.

H - HARMONIZE WISDOM WITH RESPONSE

Core Action: Use emotional information as guidance

Quick Steps:

- Developing individualized strategies for various emotions.
- Choosing conscious responses over automatic reactions.
- Asking yourself, "How can I respond from wisdom rather than reaction?"

Response Strategies by Emotion:

Emotion	Message	Wise Response
Anger	"Boundary violation"	Address the issue directly
Sadness	"Something valuable is ending."	Honor the loss, stay open to new
Fear	"Unknown territory"	Gather information, prepare appropriately
Anxiety	"This matters to me."	Take appropriate action or preparation
Joy	"This aligns with my authentic nature."	Embrace while maintaining balance
Frustration	"Current approach isn't working."	Try a different strategy or seek support

E - EMBODY NATURAL FREEDOM

Core Action: Emotional freedom should be our natural way of living.

Quick Steps:

• Integrate practices more naturally into life.

• Be confident without spiritual performance.

• Ask the question, "How can I live from this freedom naturally?"

Integration Reminders: You cannot be perfect. You cannot maintain peak states. You simply have to remember that emotional freedom is your natural state, temporarily obscured by life's challenges.

Morning Coffee

R - RADIATE AUTHENTIC PRESENCE

Core Action: Model healthy emotional expression naturally.

Quick Steps:

• Provide support to others without taking on their emotions.

• Create a safe space through your genuine presence.

• Ask: "How can I be authentically present with others?"

Presence Practices: Listen without trying to fix. Share your experience without preaching. Stay centered in your emotions as you support. Remember: authentic presence is the best gift you can give.

Emergency Emotional Weather Alerts

When all that you are is overwhelmed:

• Find a private space, if possible

• Place both hands on one's heart

• Say to yourself, "This feeling is temporary weather."

• Use the 4-7-8 breathing method (inhale for 4, hold for 7, and release the breath through the mouth for 8)

• Return when ready to step W (Witness)

When you feel that emotions are just too intense:

• No emotion has ever actually caused harm to anyone

• It will pass that intensity naturally

• Never do anything else but witness and allow

• Upon necessity, seek support

When you feel emotionally numb:

• Anxiety with numbness is also considered emotional weather

- Don't force the feeling; simply witness the absence
- Numbness usually serves as a precursor to the natural movement of emotions
- Practice self-compassion gently

Evening Reflection

- What emotional weather did I experience today?
- How did I work with challenging emotions?
- What did my emotions teach me today?

Quick Workplace Applications:

Before Important Meetings:

- 5-second pause + body scan
- Accept any nervousness or excitement you may feel.
- Set intention to respond from a place of wisdom rather than reactivity

When Receiving Criticism:

- Take notice of the impulse to defend and ask the Academy not to act on it immediately
- Explore the valid message in that feedback
- Acknowledge your emotions but choose a constructive response

During Conflict:

- Observe your emotional weather, but don't allow it to control you
- Use the emotions to help you understand what truly matters to you

- Respond with the center of your heart and values and not from your triggers

When Overwhelmed with Deadlines:

- Acknowledge your stress without judging yourself

- Take a look at what the feeling of overwhelm indicates about your current priorities and boundaries

- Use that emotional insight to guide your decisions on task management

APPENDIX C

Daily Practice Integration Checklist

Sustainable change occurs through consistent, small acts, rather than dramatic overhauls. This checklist will help you include the WEATHER Method in your daily life without added stress or pressure to perform spiritually.

Week 1: Foundation Building

Daily Core Practices (Choose 2-3):

• Take one conscious breath before drinking coffee

• Notice one's emotional weather during one routine activity, e.g., brushing teeth, taking a shower, or walking to work.

• Use the five-second pause before responding 1 time in an interaction deemed challenging

• Name one scattered emotion you are feeling without trying to alter it

• Practice the body scan for 30 seconds

Weekly Foundation Goals:

- Complete 5 times after emotional check-ins, morning/midday/evening questions

- Saying, "This [emotion] is welcome here," at least 3 times.

- Notice with three emotional patterns/triggers without judgment

- Use the quick reference guide during two emotional storms

Weekly Reflection Questions:

- What did I notice about my emotional patterns this week?

- Which WEATHER Method felt the most natural or spontaneous?

- Where was I resisting, and what might this resistance say to me?

- How did ordinary awareness moments come about?

Week 2: Deepening Awareness

Daily Core Practices (Choose 3-4):

- Complete a morning emotional weather check-in

- Practice W (Witness) during two emotional episodes

- Use E (Explore) to investigate one emotional trigger

- Apply A (Accept) to 1 difficult feeling without trying to set it right

- Notice at least three automatic emotional reactions in different contexts

Weekly Awareness Goals:

- Track emotional weather patterns for five continuous days.

- Practice full WEATHER during two challenging situations.

- Pinpoint your three primary emotional triggers and your usual reactions.

- Share your emotional weather with a trusted friend or family member.

Integration Challenges:

- Using the WEATHER Method during work stress

- Practicing acceptance of emotions during a family situation

- Applying the framework in worrying about finances

- Noticing emotional weather while watching news or browsing social media

Week 3: Flowing

Daily Core Practices (Choose 4-5):

- Completing morning prep questions completely

- Practicing T (Transition) by letting one feeling move on naturally

- Practicing H (Harmonize) to make one decision based on emotional wisdom

- Practicing E (Embody) to act from emotional freedom in one situation

- Completing midday assessment questions

Weekly Flow Goals:

- Experiencing natural emotional movement without forcing in 3 situations

- Making two decisions based on emotional information

- Noticing the difference between reacting and responding in 4 interactions

- Practicing patience in emotional timing through 2 difficult instances

Advanced Work:

- Help someone else through their emotional weather without taking it upon yourself

- Keep your emotional center while standing inside a storm of somebody else

- Use R (Radiate) as a way to ensure emotional safety for someone

- Practice emotional authenticity and not spiritual performance

Week 4: Natural Integration

Daily Core Practices (Choose 5-6):

- Carry out one complete weather check-in cycle daily

- Use the WEATHER Method in everyday interaction 3 times during emotional episodes

- Conduct all seven steps flawlessly in one challenging situation

- Authentic sharing of emotional wisdom with others

- Hold emotional freedom as default

Weekly Integration Goals:

- Experience emotional freedom naturally rather than consciously working for it

- Handle setbacks with self-compassion, not spiritual judgment

- Help others with their emotional well-being without coming off as preachy or a fixer type

- Integrate seamlessly so the practice becomes unconscious competence

Mastery Indicators:

- Cases of emotional overwhelm are scattered and fleeting
- One naturally witnesses emotions in the air, absent from being sucked into them
- Difficult emotions become information, not problems
- Others could sense your emotional stability and presence
- In the matter of decision-making, you usually use your wisdom of emotions
- Spiritually searching shall now be a natural being

Maintenance Practices Monthly

Weekly Reviews:

- Check which steps of the WEATHER Method come easiest to you
- Observe resistance still experienced in some areas
- Celebrate your progress, i.e., without spiritual perfectionism
- Change what you practice depending on what works

Deep Practices Monthly:

- Analyze your general emotional patterns over this past month
- Update your more recent strategies of response
- Note new emotional weather patterns
- Work on ways to improve your integration

Supporting Feedback:

- Meet with others who are also practicing emotional awareness
- Continue with your study of emotional intelligence
- Seeking the appropriate help-if-you-need-it will be encouraged

- Remembering: mastery is a journey, not an arrival

Workplace Integration Checklist:

Daily Professional Practices:

- Count to five before answering difficult emails

- Practice emotional weather awareness at team meetings

- Practice the WEATHER Method in one challenging interaction with a colleague

- Undertake one work-related decision using emotional intelligence

Weekly Professional Goals:

- Use emotional wisdom once in a workplace conflict

- Share emotional insights with colleagues as appropriate

- Refine healthy boundaries using emotional information

- Apply authentic presence during performance discussions

Monthly Professional Development:

- Evaluate the effects of emotional freedom on your working relationships

- Become aware of any changes in your style of leadership or collaboration

- Assess how it influences professional decision making

- Select and evaluate some areas for developing workplace practice using emotional intelligence.

APPENDIX D

Emotional Weather Pattern Tracker

Knowing your emotional climate will help you work with patterns rather than against them. This tracker promotes self-awareness by simply observing occurrences rather than condemning them with judgments or further analysis.

How to Use This Tracker

Daily Tracking Method: Record your observations without attempting to modify, analyze, or improve anything. Think of yourself as a weather meteorologist—simply noting what is going on in your emotional atmosphere.

Tracking Categories:

Weather Type: What emotion(s) are you experiencing?

- Clear (calm, peaceful, content)
- Partly cloudy (mild concern, slight agitation, minor worry)
- Cloudy (frustrated, disappointed, mildly sad)
- Stormy (angry, highly anxious, deeply sad)

- Fog (confused, uncertain, emotionally unclear)
- Sunny (joyful, excited, optimistic)
- Windy (restless, scattered, changeable)

Weather Intensity: Rate on a scale of 1 to 5.

- 1: Barely noticeable
- 2: Mild awareness
- 3: Moderate presence
- 4: Strong influence
- 5: Overwhelming intensity

Weather Duration: How long did this emotional weather last?

- Passing shower (minutes)
- Brief storm (1-2 hours)

Weather Triggers: What seemed to stand in the way of this emotional climate?

- Work situations
- Relationship interactions
- Money concerns
- Health issues
- News/media consumption
- Sleep patterns
- Physical environment
- Spiritual practices
- Social situations
- Internal thoughts/memories

Weather Responses: How did you work with this emotional weather?

- Observed without reaction
- Explored with curiosity
- Accepted without any resistance
- Allowed movement to happen naturally
- Used wisdom in response
- Embraced freedom naturally
- Shared with honesty
- Struggled or resisted
- Got swept up in it
- Attempted to force a change

Weekly Weather Patterns

Week of: _____

Daily Weather Log:

Day	Weather Type	Intensity	Duration	Triggers	Response
Monday					
Tuesday					
Wednesday					
Thursday					
Friday					
Saturday					
Sunday					

Weekly Weather Summary:

Most commonly experienced weather: _____

Most difficult weather: _____

Most prolific set-up: _____

The clash: _____

Further patterns: _____

Monthly Weather Climate Review

Month of: _____

Overall Emotional Climate: Describe your general emotional atmosphere for this month. Was it mostly stable, highly variable, predominantly one type of weather, or seasonal?

Recurring Weather Systems: What kind of pattern appeared over and over? Observe these without passing judgment-these are just your current weather tendencies.

Trigger Patterns: Which situations or circumstances most consistently brought about changes in your emotional weather? What does this say about your present life conditions?

Evolving Responses: How did your treatment of emotional weather change over this month? In what areas did you strengthen, and which remained a challenge?

Weather Forecast: What emotional weather might you expect over the next month based on your past experiences? How can you prepare for it?

Seasonal Emotional Weather Tracking

Season: _____

Seasonal Pattern: Some people experience seasonal mood swings. Track how your emotional weather aligns with:

- Time of the Year
- Weather Conditions
- Hours of Daylight
- Socio-Cultural Events
- Anniversary Dates
- Life Transitions

Long-period Weather Cycles: Watch for emotional patterns that span several weeks or months instead of days:

- Cycles of energy levels
- Variations in moods
- Changes in stress tolerance
- Fluctuations in social needs
- Periods of spiritual openness

Higher-Level Weather Awareness

Micro-Weather Tracking: For higher-level awareness, at times, track emotional weather by the hour during unusually interesting or challenging days:

Hour-by-Hour Weather on [Date]: _____

Time	Weather	Intensity	Trigger	Response
6 AM				
8 AM				
10 AM				
12 PM				
2 PM				
4 PM				
6 PM				
8 PM				
10 PM				

Weather Prediction Practice: With increased awareness of your patterns, go ahead and practice your emotional weather forecasting:

- What emotional weather might arise from tomorrow's schedule?
- How can you go about preparing for likely weather patterns?
- Which WEATHER Method step could be most useful?

Interpersonal Weather Tracking: Attend to how one's emotional weather interacts with others:

- How does family emotional weather affect you?
- What's your emotional weather like in different social situations?
- How do you influence others' emotional climates?

Weather Wisdom Integration: Use your tracking data to devise strategies that are beneficial to your situation:

- Which steps of the WEATHER Method seem to be most useful for your usual patterns?
- What changes in either environment or lifestyle would help your emotional well-being?

- What can you do with emotional weather information to improve your decision-making?

Progress Indicators

Weekly Progress Markers:

- Better awareness of subtle emotional shifts

- Quicker recovery from emotional storms

- More spontaneous use of WEATHER Method steps

- Greater confidence with difficult emotions

- Better emotional vocabulary and description

Monthly Progress Markers:

- Reduced overall emotional reactivity

- Better Prediction of emotional weather patterns

- More skillful Response to challenging emotions

- Heightened emotional resilience and stability

- Fluent Integration of emotional wisdom into everyday life

Remember: You are not your weather. These patterns of weather are atmospheric conditions in the vast space of your being. They provide information but cannot define your essence.

The aim is not to control your emotional weather but rather to cultivate the wisdom and skills to work with whatever weather is there. In other words, just as meteorologists study weather patterns to assist communities in adequately preparing for response, you study your emotional patterns to live in greater freedom and authenticity.

Your observing of emotional weather becomes a meditation on impermanence; it becomes practice in acceptance and a resource for developing the kind of emotional mastery that allows spiritual freedom to arise effortlessly through mundane moments.

Now, with the appendices, you have everything you need to practically apply the WEATHER Method, rather than just soaking up inspiration. These tools ensure that your journey to escaping an ocean of emotions and toward spiritual freedom continues long after you've finished reading, making emotional mastery your default way of being, not a spiritual achievement to be cherished.

As you forge ahead in this freedom, remember: every ordinary moment—your morning coffee, a tough conversation, a burst of joy, or stretches of sadness—holds the potential for awakening that mystics have tapped into throughout history. The difference lies not in the moments themselves but in how you engage them with the weathered wisdom grounded in your changing."

NOTES

Chapter 2: The Ordinary Miracle

1. Needs: Kahneman, D. (1999). Objective happiness. In D. Kahneman, E. Diener, & N. Schwarz (Eds.), *Well-being: The foundations of hedonic psychology* (pp. 3-25). Russell Sage Foundation.
2. Goodreads. (2025, March 28). Quote by Rumi: "Let yourself be silently drawn by the strange pull of what you really love. It will not lead you astray." https://www.goodreads.com/quotes/541057-let-yourself-be-silently-drawn-by-the-strange-pull-of
3. Ferguson, A. (2023, August 30). How tea became the symbol of enlightenment. *Tricycle: The Buddhist Review*. https://tricycle.org/trikedaily/consider-source-how-did-tea-come-symbolize-enlightenment
4. Quintiliani, A. R. (2017). How does Thich Nhat Hanh drink a cup of tea? *Mindful Happiness*. Retrieved from https://mindfulhappiness.org/2017/thich-nhat-hanh-drink-cup-tea/

Chapter 3: The WEATHER Method Revealed

1. Taylor, J. B. (2008). My stroke of insight: A brain scientist's personal journey. Viking.

www.ingramcontent.com/pod-product-compliance
Lightning Source LLC
Chambersburg PA
CBHW022013290426
44109CB00015B/1155